# THE REAGAN I KNEW

# Also by William F. Buckley Jr.

God and Man at Yale (1951)

McCarthy and His Enemies,
co-authored with L. Brent Bozell Jr.
(1954)

Up from Liberalism (1959)

The Committee and Its Critics (ed.)
(1962)

Rumbles Left and Right (1963)

The Unmaking of a Mayor (1966)

The Jeweler's Eye (1968)

Odyssey of a Friend,
by Whittaker Chambers, introduction
and notes by WFB (1969)

The Governor Listeth (1970)

Did You Ever See a Dream Walking?
(ed.) (1970)

Cruising Speed (1971)

Inveighing We Will Go (1972)

Four Reforms (1973)

United Nations Journal (1974)

Execution Eve (1975)

* Saving the Queen (1976)

Airborne (1976)

* Stained Glass (1978)

A Hymnal (1978)

* Who's on First (1980)

* Marco Polo, If You Can (1982)

Atlantic High (1982)

Overdrive (1983)

* The Story of Henri Tod (1984)

* See You Later Alligator (1985)

* The Temptation of Wilfred
Malachey (1985)

Right Reason, edited by Richard
Brookhiser (1985)

* High Jinx (1986)

Racing through Paradise (1987)

* Mongoose, R.I.P. (1988)

Keeping the Tablets, co-edited with
Charles R. Kesler (1988)

On the Firing Line (1989)

Gratitude (1990)

* Tucker's Last Stand (1990)

Windfall (1992)

In Search of Anti-Semitism (1992)

Happy Days Were Here Again,
edited by Patricia Bozell (1993)

* A Very Private Plot (1994)

* The Blackford Oakes Reader
(1995)

* Brothers No More (1995)

Buckley: The Right Word, edited by
Samuel S. Vaughan (1996)

The Lexicon (1996)

Nearer, My God (1997)

* The Redhunter (1999)

Let Us Talk of Many Things (2000)

* Spytime (2000)

* Elvis in the Morning (2001)

* Nuremberg (2002)

* Getting It Right (2003)

The Fall of the Berlin Wall (2004)

Miles Gone By (2004)

* Last Call for Blackford Oakes
(2005)

* The Rake (2007)

Cancel Your Own Goddam
Subscription (2007)

Flying High: Remembering Barry
Goldwater (2008)

* FICTION

# The Reagan I Knew

## WILLIAM F. BUCKLEY JR.

BASIC
BOOKS

A Member of the Perseus Books Group
*New York*

Copyright © 2008 by the Estate of William F. Buckley Jr.
Published by Basic Books
A Member of the Perseus Books Group

Books published by Basic Books are available at special
discounts for bulk purchases in the United States by
corporations, institutions, and other organizations.
For more information, please contact the
Special Markets Department at the Perseus Books Group,
2300 Chestnut Street, Suite 200, Philadelphia, PA 19103,
or call (800) 810-4145, ext. 5000, or e-mail
special.markets@perseusbooks.com.

Designed by Timm Bryson

Library of Congress Cataloging-in-Publication Data

Buckley, William F. (William Frank), 1925–2008.
    The Reagan I knew / William F. Buckley, Jr.
        p. cm.
    ISBN 978-0-465-00926-8 (alk. paper)
1. Reagan, Ronald. 2. Reagan, Ronald—Friends and
associates. 3. Presidents—United States—Biography. 4.
Buckley, William F. (William Frank), 1925  2008. I. Title.
E877.B83 2008
973.927092—dc22
[B]
                                        2008032557

*To my grandchildren, Caitlin Gregg Buckley and William Conor Buckley*

# CONTENTS

# CONTENTS

# CONTENTS

# FOREWORD

This is my father's fifty-fifth and, inasmuch as he died while writing it, one might suppose final book. I put it this way not to be coy, but because there seems to be a possibility, given the enthusiasm in various publishing quarters, of bringing out another collection of his articles. So this might turn out *not* to be his last book. At the time he died, his book *Cancel Your Own Goddam Subscription* (what a great title) had recently come out. As I type these words, his book on Barry Goldwater, *Flying High*, has just been published. And now this, his memoir of his friendship with Ronald Reagan is—*évidemment*, as WFB would say in French—being published. My father writes more books dead than some authors do alive.

This book was substantially completed before he was struck down the morning of February 27, 2008, at his desk in his study in Stamford. He had begun work on it the previous fall, in the company of Danilo Petranovich, an engaging and very bright Yale political science PhD. They had gone together to a rented house on the ocean in Fort Lauderdale over December–January, and were putting the final touches on it when he died. The book was left in good hands with Danilo, my father's last protégé, in a very long line of protégés. Among Pup's many talents was Pied Pipership: the list of young people whom he mentored—to use a verb that would appall him—at *National Review* or as literary assistants might well fill out the pages of this book.

The idea for this book arose from the previous book, on Goldwater. This one is a natural, even eerily fitting, coda to my father's oeuvre. WFB was, inarguably, the founder and *primum mobile* of modern American conservatism. His biographer, Sam Tanenhaus, has written that his first book, *God and Man at Yale*, published in 1951, "contained the seeds of a movement." As it has been put, again and again, if it hadn't been for Buckley, there wouldn't have been Goldwater, and without Goldwater, there wouldn't have been Reagan. How apt, then, that his last book should be about the man whose career he in a sense enabled.

Ronald Reagan was an elusive personality. Indeed, his biographer, Edmund Morris, found him so elusive that he resorted, in his masterly but controversial book *Dutch*, to confecting an imaginary character in an attempt to deconstruct his subject. But though Reagan tended, famously, to shy from personal intimacy, I think it's entirely possible that Pup may have gotten as close to him as one could. It was a true friendship. WFB was *very* close to Nancy Reagan, as the letters between them here will show. And at various points, Pup became a mentor (that awful word again) to the Reagan children, Patti and Ron Jr.

I first met Reagan when Pup took me along with him to California in 1967, to do several *Firing Line* tapings. Honesty compels me to say that for this fourteen-year-old, the real excitement of the trip was the *Firing Line* taping not with the new governor of California but with Robert Vaughn, star of *The Man from U.N.C.L.E.* Vaughn was at the time an aspirant liberal eminence, which vocation apparently was short-lived.

The Reagans gave a cocktail party for Pup at the governor's mansion. *Le tout* Sacramento turned out. I was swiftly ignored amidst the sea of grown-ups and at one point wandered out into the garden and sat down by myself. A few moments later, I sensed the presence of someone next to me and, turning, saw the Governor of California, movie-star handsome and big, in a white jacket. He had seen me wander off and, sensing that I must be feeling a bit lost and out of place, had come out to talk. I never forgot that gesture. If Reagan was capable of reticence, he was also capable of graciousness. In that capacity, he and WFB were made for each other.

Fifteen years later, completely by accident (I had written something in *Esquire* that had impressed George H. W. Bush's press secretary), I found myself working in Ronald Reagan's White House. The Reagans kindly invited me to the odd social occasion. On one of these, I very nearly made a faux pas of national proportion.

The invitation was for dinner in the residence upstairs and a movie afterward. I had a big speech to write for Bush that night, and pleaded urgently with Muffie Brandon, Mrs. Reagan's social secretary, to be excused from the movie. She tsk-tsked but said all right, but I must be discreet about leaving. I said of course. As I made my stealthy exit just before the lights went down in the family theater, I rounded a corner in the hallway and bumped smack into—Ronald Reagan, who was returning either from the men's room or from ordering a richly deserved missile strike on some Mideastern despot.

He smiled that 1,000-watt smile and regarded me with a look of mild surprise. "Where are you going?" he said. "We're about to start the movie."

"Uh," I dissembled, "just, uh, going to the men's room, sir. I'll be right there. Go ahead and start without me."

He smiled and went off, phalanxed by Secret Service, including Tim McCarthy, who a few months earlier had interposed himself between the President and John Hinckley.

I made my way down the long corridor in the basement and was about to exit the White House when I heard behind me a sibilant and very stressed *"Psssst!"*

Looking back, I saw Muffie Brandon, frantically gesticulating. "He just announced to everyone that we weren't going to start without you."

*Oh my God.* I skulked back, Muffie more or less leading me by the ear, to find fifty guests glowering at me, and my seat saved—in the front row, next to the President and Mrs. Reagan.

I experienced dozens of such random acts of grace and favor during my time at the White House. Looking back on it, I realize— not that I didn't at the time—that these were reciprocations for the kindnesses that Pup had shown to the Reagans' children.

A few years later, in 1985, I found myself—again, accidentally—ghost-writing David Stockman's memoirs, under furious deadline pressure. (I use the term "ghost-writing" in the narrowly technical sense: my job was to turn a mountain—yea, a veritable Kilimanjaro—of manuscript into readable English.) There was a certain piquancy to this assignment, inasmuch as David Stockman had become hugely famous for an act of impertinence to Reagan while serving as his budget director. But (a)

Stockman's beef was never *ad hominem* against Reagan; and anyway (b) I needed the dough.

In the midst of this death march fell *National Review*'s gala 30th anniversary dinner at the Plaza in New York. I pleaded with Pup that I couldn't attend—I barely had time to eat meals. No, he insisted, you have to be there, as he put it somewhat mysteriously, *for reasons that will become apparent.* I grumpily assented—Pup wasn't someone you could, really, say no to. (That's another story.)

So I went, and was seated right above the podium when he gave the speech that is reproduced here. Looking back on that moment, on those two amazing men, I reflect that, yes, the blood of the fathers truly did run strong.

*Christopher Buckley*
*Washington, D.C.*
*May 2008*

# INTRODUCTION

The bulk of this book was written in Fort Lauderdale, Florida. There, William F. Buckley Jr. and I spent six weeks researching, discussing, writing, and editing the chapters you will find here.

This is a story of Ronald Reagan and his contribution to American conservative politics. Reagan was, in Buckley's—and many others'—view, *the* great conservative politician of the twentieth century, and it is as such, as Buckley made clear throughout our collaboration, that he should be scrutinized.

The basic Reagan narrative is pretty well known by now. There are superb volumes outlining Reagan's political ascent, his time in office, his towering impact on the nation and the world. What is not as well known is the particular relationship Reagan had with one of the most important architects of the modern conservative Weltanschauung (to use a word he himself might have used). Buckley and Reagan met while Reagan was still a Democrat and Buckley already a renowned conservative commentator, a phenomenon of the new Right. In the months and years after this first encounter, as Reagan's star rose (and rose), his political philosophy crystallized and his embrace of the conservative outlook, resuscitated by Buckley in post–New Deal America, became as complete as one can expect from a political leader. Reagan was never a theorist within the conservative movement, but he became the greatest expositor of the conservative cause in American politics.

This book traces the arc of Reagan's political career through the prism of Buckley's contacts with him, and as such is the story of the friendship between the two great figures of the modern American Right: the movement's articulator and its star. Buckley's analysis of Reagan's basic positions and policies falls under three headings: foreign policy (nuclear deterrence vis-à-vis the Soviet Union), the economy (and the bloated federal government), and federalism (the issue of states' rights, or separation of powers, as Bill often preferred to phrase it). Thus the leading issues of the day are limned through an account of the friendship of "Bill" and "Ron" over more than three decades.

Reagan shied from drawing back the curtain on his private life. The intimate glimpses we get here should prove interesting to even the most conversant Reagan and Buckley fans.

As to the public Reagan, this book reproduces one of the most compelling speeches ever delivered by WFB. In Reagan's presence, toward the end of *National Review*'s 30th Anniversary celebration, Buckley gave stirring, distinctly non-ambiguist remarks about confronting the Soviet Union in the nuclear age. If the Soviets were to launch a strike against us, he said, it would be met with resolute determination on our part, and would prove to be suicidal for their regime. And yet, Buckley asks in retrospect, if it had come to that, *would* Reagan actually have launched missiles?

"I was into some heavy stuff in those days," Buckley reflected in one of our Fort Lauderdale talks. Examining the heavy stuff, he crafted a fictional (but well founded on personal knowledge) conversation between Clare Boothe Luce, godmother (if you will) of the vast right-wing conspiracy, and Defense Secretary Caspar Weinberger, intended to reveal Reagan's thinking on nuclear weapons. The President, we hear, detests nuclear weapons and is uncomfortable discussing doomsday scenarios with his inner circle. The national security experts are astonished by his philosophical and practical orientation on this most serious of issues. What is ultimately revealed by these exchanges, however, is that the intuition of Ronald Reagan was superior to that of the sophisticates, in both the conservative and the liberal worlds.

The discussion of Reagan's economic policies deals primarily with the size of government and the budget deficit, dominant themes of the 1980s. Buckley reconstructs some of the most significant debates over Reaganomics. Reagan, of course, had promised to cut the size of government, and yet the budget deficit nearly doubled during his tenure. Was this an overt submission to increased government, or a defeat at the hands of forces he could not control? In a "self-interrogation"—a Buckley specialty, which he first deployed in his 1966 classic, *The Unmaking of a Mayor*—the author attempts to sort out difficulties associated with Reagan's "economic revolution." We also revisit the drama over David Stockman, Reagan's young and controversial budget director, and listen in on some of the advice Reagan received from Buckley on handling the whole situation.

"Mr. Reagan," Buckley once wrote, "has accomplished a great deal, but perhaps he will be remembered by our great-grandchildren for two reasons: the first, that he presided over the counterrevolution against the creeping idea that the state has a pre-emptive right to the production of its citizens; and, second, that he is almost certainly the nicest man who ever occupied the White House."

We see both of those Reagans in this book. There are excerpts from several of the *Firing Line* episodes in which Reagan appeared. The first is in 1967: Buckley and Reagan are carefully parsing the vital issue of federalism in Great Society America. Questions about the proper scope of government dominate the conversation, but there are also forays into related aspects of American politics and society. The reader will get a sense of Buckley's formidable intellect and legendary wit, as well as Reagan's instinctive grasp of the American character and his winning style of humor.

The "nice Reagan" is present throughout this book. Whether he is charming his listeners with stories or welcoming Truman Capote to the California death house, coming up with a wisecrack or gracefully recovering after the attempt on his life, the private Reagan is almost always sunny and positive. He is always confident about the most important matter, the virtue of the American character, big-hearted and open, hard-working and determined. The portrait we get here reveals a warm and captivating soul, a loyal friend, and a loving husband. We also see an overwhelmed and, at times, aloof father. Buckley writes candidly about the relations within the Reagan family. He had a warm relationship with both Patti and Ron Jr. going back to their early days, as is apparent from his correspondence with Patti while she was at boarding school, and from Ron Jr.'s visits with the Buckleys in Connecticut and New York City. Buckley's role, it becomes apparent, went beyond that of a mentor to Reagan in matters of political philosophy; he was also a close family friend and counselor.

The Reagan with whom Buckley had, arguably, the most intimate relationship was Nancy. They delighted in each other's company from the start. Nancy enjoyed WFB's wordplay. In the first letter she writes to him, she tells him that she is waiting for the right time to drop the recently assimilated term "Zeitgeist" into her conversation and amaze all her friends. Buckley writes to her with commiseration over the difficulties of life in public office. There is also a running joke that they are soon to meet at Sammy's Bar in Casablanca. "Travel lightly, and don't leave a forwarding address," he advises her.

Also included in this book are selections from the captivating and illuminating correspondence between WFB and Ronald Reagan, stretching over the thirty-plus years of their friendship. These letters offer the reader a glimpse into the open and wide-ranging nature of the association between these two men. There are high-level foreign-policy analyses and discussions of Supreme Court nominees; advice on running campaigns and managing presidential staff; plans for celebrations at the Plaza Hotel and vacations in Barbados; expressions of support for the Reagan children in their pursuit of dance and poetry; and, throughout the years of Reagan's presidency, regular reports on Buckley's secret mission as ambassador to Afghanistan. Disagreements, even profound ones, were part of their relationship. One need not look further than their public debate over the Panama Canal, or their private exchanges on disarmament negotiations with the Soviets, to see that Reagan and Buckley did not see eye to eye on everything. But, as the letters reveal, no matter what the occasion or the argument, these two giants of American conservatism engaged each other with deep mutual respect and solicitude for their unique and consequential friendship.

What WFB said in describing his memoir of Barry Goldwater holds true for this one as well: The material in this book is "factually reliable." While many of the conversations are reported from memory and probably are not word-for-word accurate, there are no distortions. No thought, as he put it, is "engrafted" onto anyone so as to alter the subject's character, inclinations, or habits of speech.

Assisting Bill Buckley with this book has been the most stimulating work experience I have ever had. Buckley was a brilliant writer and a penetrating and wide-ranging thinker. He organized his ideas by putting them on paper immediately. Whenever we needed to change the direction of the narrative or commence a new chapter, Buckley would open another WordStar file and start outlining. He thought best by writing things out. Sometimes I would produce a first draft or provide some background material for a chapter, but when he took the lead, he insisted I not read the material until he had fully drafted it. Once an episode was finished, he would almost never go back to it, intending to postpone any revisions until the whole draft was completed.

I liked his style. I adjusted quickly to his routine, and we produced good material on a daily basis. But, as Bill pointed out to me on more than a few occasions, this was not the pace he was used to from his "cruising speed" days. He was apologetic about this, seemingly unaware of how impressed I was both with his work ethic and with his creative output. In spite of his deteriorating health, Buckley sustained a productive work schedule to the very end, all the while continuing to entertain old friends and new acquaintances. As he once said about Ronald Reagan, so with Bill Buckley, the show must go on.

Over the months we worked on this book we saw each other or spoke on the phone almost every day. I watched and learned from him how to craft an argument, introduce a character, enliven a scene, provoke the reader. I loved our conversations, and I thrilled at taking part in his enchanted atmosphere, which he created wherever he went. What I will remember above all, however, is his irrepressible laughter at the inevitable "potholes of life," as he put it. Bill at times suffered a great deal, and ordinary things became more difficult for this extraordinary man as time passed. But he never stopped laughing, and teasing, and having fun, and marveling at the new and the proven old. Ours was a joyful experience, and I will always be grateful to our Lord God for intertwining our lives.

*Danilo Petranovich*
*Hamden, Connecticut*
*May 2008*

# Prologue

This book is about Ronald Reagan. The public Reagan, obviously, but also, almost always, simply the Ronald Reagan I came to know. Except that he was a great public figure who moved mountains, there would be scant curiosity about him. But he became, for a while, the most prominent politician on earth. I would not, otherwise, be undertaking a book about him. However, this book is one in which the large scale of things is quite intentionally diminished or, better, maneuvered around, to make way for the cultivation of personal curiosity about someone who became a good friend.

I proceed as I do because I did know him, as a friend and, in a sense, as a tutor. I say this because Ronald Reagan had been a

PROLOGUE

liberal and an earnest Democrat, though he had moved far in our direction by the time we met. As our friendship matured, I became, simultaneously, a close friend of his wife, Nancy. And for a while, I was on companionable terms with their two children. Patti was fourteen and Ron Jr. eight when I first met them as children of the governor of California in 1967. The story there (father/children) is unconventional, and I played a minor role as a family consultant. I intend to tell that story, to the extent I know it, because it interests me as a family story that bumped into larger-than-life-size developments.

# 1

# First Meeting

In January 1961, I was hired, through my lecture agent, to give a speech in Beverly Hills to an assembly called Citizens for Better Education. Over the years I spoke frequently in the Los Angeles area, and on this occasion I followed my usual routine. When passing through Los Angeles I would stay at the home of my wife's older sister. Kathleen "Bill" Finucane had left her hometown of Vancouver, B.C., many years before to marry a California lawyer. They lived in Pasadena with their daughter, and there was always a spare room.

Bill Finucane was one of those female earth movers who run everybody's life. She had a formal job, as head of the Los Angeles Red Cross volunteer blood program. This kept her moving, and at a tempo (she rose at 5 A.M.) one would have ruled out of bounds for a woman who, at six feet tall, weighed nearly three hundred pounds. But Bill Finucane was anxious to be of service to friends and family, and this included picking me up at airports, driving me to her house, supervising my dress, driving me to my engagement, and eventually returning me to her house, where she put me up for the night.

On the evening in question, we had called for the dinner check at the restaurant across the street from the El Rodeo School Auditorium, where my talk was scheduled. The couple on their way out paused, and Ronald Reagan, with a voluptuarian smile, introduced himself and Nancy.

I had been told that Reagan would be introducing me to the assembly (mostly doctors) but had given it no thought. By 1961, he was pulling away from the Democratic assignments he had performed for over twenty years, during which time he had divorced from his first wife and remarried to the petite lady at his side. He declaimed joyfully his high anticipation for the hour ahead, and quoted and laughed over a barbed comment in my book *Up from Liberalism* at the expense of Mrs. Roosevelt.

We crossed the street and walked into a scene of some consternation. The large hall was full, but one of our hosts explained to us that the microphone was dead and the student who was supposed to have turned it on was nowhere to be found. They were happy to see Mr. Reagan. With his familiarity with stage machinery he certainly would find a means of turning on the sound.

But he did not, even after two or three minutes of trying. It appeared that nothing could be done except from the (locked) control room at balcony level at the rear of the hall. So Reagan dispatched someone to call the principal's office and see if we could get the key. Meanwhile, he undertook to appease the crowd. Raising his voice, he told a story or two and said the current difficulty illustrated the need for better education. There was a ripple of appreciation, but now the assistant returned and reported there was no answer at the principal's office. By now there were rumbles of impatience coming in from the crowd.

Reagan then walked to the side of the hall and peered through the window at the parapet running the length of the building, two stories above the traffic. His diagnosis seemed instantaneous. He was out the window, his feet on the parapet, his back to the wall, sidestepping carefully toward the control-room window. Reaching it, he thrust his elbow, breaking the glass, and disappeared into the control room. In a minute there was light in the upstairs room, and then we could hear the crackling of the newly animated microphone.

That was a dramatic first meeting, and a friendship was kindled. He was, in those days, edging his way out from the political assumptions he had grown up with as a young Democrat. He had been fighting the Communists in the Screen Actors Guild and was now looking for company on what we would call the Barry Goldwater side of the political world. He would give a famous speech a few years later urging the support of Goldwater. Goldwater didn't win, but Reagan soon found himself with a political career shaping up. A coterie of Republicans grouped about him, seeking a figure large enough to hang their shattered hopes on.

During that period I visited often, and when he confided that he was deliberating a bid for governor of California, I took to referring to him sotto voce as "Guv"—"How's the Guv doing?" I'd jest with Nancy over the phone. But I was way behind in apprehending his potential. Governor Nelson Rockefeller, at our first private meeting (at his New York apartment in January 1968), asked me how to account for the sounds beginning to come out of California—Why not Reagan for president? "There's no way," I found myself opining on politics to a man in his third term as governor of New York, "a former actor could go for president."

"Anybody who wins the California election by one million votes is presidential material," was Rockefeller's answer. Five years after our first meeting, Reagan had done just that.

"He's not even a good actor," one commentator protested. Oh?

"That, as it happens, is not true," Los Angeles sportswriter Jim Murray wrote in *Esquire* in February 1966.

Ronald Reagan was and is a very good actor, indeed. Seventy-five percent of being a good actor is voice. Only a Spencer Tracy can get away with a squeaky, unheroic timbre and Ronald Reagan has such a strong, mellifluous delivery that he was once a sports announcer—and a good one at that.

Look at it this way: he had to be a good actor. He's not handsome. There's something earnest and unromantic about him. He couldn't make the gossip columns if he eloped with the Queen of Iran. He's got all that hair and teeth. His figure is good, but no one ever asked him to take off his shirt in a movie to help the box office. He never tested for Tarzan. He drinks sparingly. He lives within his budget: no solid-gold Lincolns or Cadillacs, no champagne parties in New York hotels. You color him grey. "Ronnie is like the end of autumn," a friend confides.

What he is, is a Republican. His reading runs to tomes on tax reform. His life is as organized as a monk's. He is a homebody. His marriage is one of those the fan magazines always hold up as paragons of matrimony.

But all the things Ronald Reagan is *not* as an actor, he *is* as a politician. As a fifty-four-year-old candidate, he *is* handsome. He *is* compelling, romantic even. If you're a forty-year-old female precinct worker, Ronald Reagan is an event in your life.

# *Correspondence, 1965–1966*

January 4, 1965

Dear Bill--

Many thanks for the lovely Christmas plant you sent--it helped make everything very festive. We loved having you at our house and hope you'll let us know when you're going to be here again. . . .

I'm still waiting for just the right moment to drop Zeitgeist (sp?!) into the conversation and amaze all my friends--but so far it hasn't come--it's terribly frustrating.

Fondly,
Nancy

🙠     🙠     🙠

January 6, 1965

Dear Nancy:

The spelling is exactly right! You were sweet to write, and I'll take you up on your invitation. Why don't you consider, as an alternative, coming over and skiing with us in Gstaad? We'll be there for a

couple of months (hope to finish a book[1]). My most
cordial greetings to you both.

> As ever,
> Bill

❧        ❧        ❧

> January 14, 1965

Dear Bill--

Skiing in Gstaad?! How heavenly. I envy you but I'm
afraid I'll have to enjoy it vicariously--and look
forward to the book appearing. . . .
I alternately feel terribly brave about the whole
thing[2] and then as if I'd like to crawl into a cave
where no one could find me. I know if Ronnie does
decide to go into politics all the way I'd better get
over that. . . .

> Fondly,
> Nancy

❧        ❧        ❧

---

1. In fact, the book WFB was working on, called *The Revolt against the
Masses*, was one of the very few projects in the course of his life that he
started but never finished.

2. RR was resisting pressure from leading California Republicans to
challenge Governor Edmund "Pat" Brown in 1966, but meanwhile he had
agreed to give a number of speeches at Republican functions around the state.

February 23, 1965

Dear Bill,

I don't know whether you are back from the snows of
Switzerland, and what part of your anatomy may be
encased in plaster of Paris. I'm not a pessimist, but
it seems that all my skiing friends sport casts as
proof that they had a winter vacation. I'll hope you
don't, but if you do that it uses the smallest amount
of plaster and is the least inconvenient possible.

I just wanted to thank you for what you did with
regard to Mr. Hayes and *Esquire* magazine.[3] Probably
nothing can head off the vengeful Miss Mitford, but
I appreciate very much your trying. Maybe it will
awaken the editorial conscience of Mr. Hayes, and
he'll take a firmer grasp of his blue pencil.

Nancy sends her best.

Sincerely,
Ron

✒       ✒       ✒

December 28, 1965

Dear Bill--

Please forgive me for not writing before this to
thank you for the lovely flowers--but between
politics and Christmas, I don't know whether I'm
coming or going. . . .

---

3. Word had reached Reagan that *Esquire*, under legendary editor Harold
Hayes, the godfather of the New Journalism, had assigned Jessica Mitford to
do a portrait of Reagan. Hayes eventually rejected the portrait, and Mitford
sold it to the far-left *Ramparts*.

We loved being with you--as always--but I think I've been a good friend to all my friends long enough--they've met you now. Next time I'm going to keep your arrival a deep dark secret so we can really talk--I have a feeling we didn't scratch the surface. . . .

The announcement will be on the 4th, as I told you, and I must say my emotions are wired. I awaken early often and think, "Good God. What have we gotten ourselves into?" Well, we shall see. Don't you think you'll have to come out here sometime during the campaign for *National Review*? Please do--I want my friends around me too--not just my enemies!

> Fondly,
> Nancy

꒰         ꒰         ꒰

> Dictated in Switzerland
> Transcribed in New York
> February 18, 1966

Dear Nancy:

Goodness, answering your letter was interrupted by an emergency round trip to New York. The usual legal entanglements in re *Pauling* vs. *Buckley*.[4] It goes to

---

4. In January 1963, chemist and political activist Linus Pauling filed suit against *National Review*; its editor, WFB; and its publisher, William A. Rusher. Pauling claimed he had been libeled in an *NR* editorial titled "The Collaborators," which began, "What are we going to do about those of our fellow citizens who persist in a course of collaboration with the enemy who has sworn to bury us?" The trial began in March 1966, and the judge dismissed the suit six weeks later.

trial next week, and I shall return once more to New York to transact that ugly business.

Your letter half cheered me, half made me blue. I know what you and Ronnie are going through and only wish I could spare you some of the chaff . . .

With affectionate regards to you both,

Bill

⤝       ⤝       ⤝

July 11, 1966
Dear Bill:

Where do I find the words to say thanks for what seemed like the whole magazine devoted to me, but beyond that, for a cover yet?[5] It was very thrilling and it was most generous of you to do this in my behalf.

I'm grateful, Nancy's grateful, and why don't you come to California again so we can tell you in person?

I'm going to save that particular issue to look at in the months ahead, because I think brother Brown[6] has some good, juicy, muddy ones to throw at me and I'll need a morale booster every once in a while. I'm

---

5. The June 28 issue of *National Review* contained two articles on Reagan—one of them by old friend Morrie Ryskind (see chapter 2)—and a cover portrait, captioned "The Future of Ronald Reagan."

6. Governor Brown's campaign became famous for the TV ad in which Brown, talking with some elementary-school children, told a little black girl, "You know I'm running against an actor. Remember this: You know who shot Abraham Lincoln, don't you?" When the children giggled nervously, Brown said, "An actor shot Lincoln."

going to get it just looking at that issue of
*National Review.*

Seriously, we do hope you have another date of some kind in California, soon. It would be so good to see you again.

Again, my heartfelt thanks.

Best regards,
Ron

᠑       ᠑       ᠑

NOVEMBER 7, 1966

AM THINKING OF YOU AND RONNIE FULLY CONFIDENT. IF YOU LOSE YOU CAN AT LEAST TAKE PRIDE IN THE CAMPAIGN YOU WAGED AND IN THE HOPE YOU GAVE TO SO MANY OF US.

—BILL

᠑       ᠑       ᠑

RONALD REAGAN
GOVERNOR-ELECT
STATE OF CALIFORNIA

December 7, 1966

Dear Bill:

The tumult and shouting have ended, but I'm now suffering from the fallout. I thought I'd be happy to see the campaign close, but either I miss the sawdust trail or I'm getting hit over the head too often with all that has to be done.

Have you any idea how many people want to serve the State of California? But beyond that, I'm finding out

all of my charges against the present Administration
were understatements. This state, if it was a
private business, would have a padlock on the door
and be in the hands of receivers. It is fantastic
from my present vantage point to discover what
really faces one when the chance comes to put order
into the chaos our little liberal playmates have
created.

Meanwhile, the old Guv is busily appointing
judges, some 50 of them in these closing hours,
including some whose records occupy many many pages
in House Un-American Activities Committee reports.
But, so much for that.

What I really set out to write was a heartfelt
thank you for kind words spoken and written, for
morale-building when morale was low, particularly
morale-building for Nancy. Seriously, I want you to
know I'm deeply grateful.

Nancy tells me you will be out here in the near
future. I hope we'll have a chance to get together.
Perhaps then I can tell you better how really
grateful I am.

Best regards,
Ron

# 2

# Visiting the Reagans
# in California

When Nancy Reagan was shown the house in Sacramento in which California sheltered its governor, she smiled (if that is the right word for it) and announced that she would not be caught dead "in that firetrap." The dwelling, constructed in 1877, the sometime home of Governors George Pardee, Hiram Johnson, and Earl Warren, was a Victorian Gothic pile in poor repair, located on a street heavy with truck traffic. The Reagans found a modern, habitable house in a wealthy suburb, and proceeded to install themselves in it, with Patti and Ron Jr.

I went to California from time to time on the lecture circuit, and to film episodes of my television show, *Firing Line*. The first time Ronald Reagan taped a *Firing Line* with me was on July 6 in the first year of his term. This is a date of symbolic importance to us—July 6 is Nancy's birthday, and my own wedding anniversary. Moreover, I had invited along, on this television jaunt, my son, Christopher, then fourteen years old and a student at a cloistered Benedictine New England boarding school.

I remember reaching the peak of paternal exasperation on the westbound flight the day before. Christopher was seated at the side of his father. He watched attentively that afternoon's movie. He then started listening to music, or what passed for music with his generation. After two or three hours of this, my frustration broke out. I turned to my son and asked in the heaviest sarcasm I could come up with, "Christopher, have you *ever* read a book?"

He had adjusted his earphone only just enough to let my words into his hearing. Now he put the earphone back in place and said, "Yeah. *Treasure Island.*"

The tapings scheduled for me on July 6 would be with Ronald Reagan, freshly commissioned as governor of California, and after that with Groucho Marx, sovereign comedian of the age. I lunched in Los Angeles that day with Groucho and Morrie Ryskind, a staunch supporter of *National Review* from the beginning and the scriptwriter for Groucho's *A Night at the Opera*. It dismayed but did not surprise me that Christopher elected to eat his lunch alone, sheltered from his father and those boring old men.

The next day we were in Sacramento. I visited the governor's office, and felt well protected in the heavy wooden sanctuary. I told Reagan that I had a diplomatic commission in hand. Two weeks earlier, I had found myself cheek by jowl with Jesse Unruh, the all-powerful Speaker of the California Assembly. After dinner he took me aside. "Would you believe it," he asked, "that in the six months Reagan has been in office, I have *not once* been asked to his house, or received a phone call from him?"

I promised to relay his concern to the governor, who, on being told of it, said, "Jesse is on the other side. What's the point in letting him say that he has spoken with the governor about this problem and that problem? If he wants to cooperate with me, he can do that, any time. Doesn't need to be over drinks." He gave me his half smile, with which I had become familiar. It signified no more, I would learn, than that he saw no reason to discard his air of general benevolence. He was telling me that Jesse Unruh ran the California legislature, but Ronald Reagan ran the executive branch, and no constitutional reconciliation would alter this, so why go through the motions? When, a decade and a half later, he served in the White House, he quite often did undertake to go through motions that didn't promise success—or, for that matter, bring success.

The Reagans were giving a garden party that afternoon. We left the office and drove to their home, where they were expecting two hundred guests. The festivities were on the lawn—food and drink and music and political talk. Christopher was spirited away by the Reagan children, Patti, who was his own age, fourteen, and Ron Jr., age eight. They disappeared into the house, on the assumption, probably, that the older folk were more boring than even Groucho Marx.

# 3

# Is It Possible to Be a Good Governor?

I began that first *Firing Line* conversation with Ronald Reagan by saying:

> The purpose of this program is to ask whether it is possible to be a good governor. By that I mean this: Are we now so dependent on the federal government that the individual state is left without the scope to make its own crucial decisions?
>
> I'd like to begin by asking you, Governor Reagan, this: Isn't the individual state, in the matter of taxation, required to make do with what amounts to the leftovers, it being the right of

Congress freely to exercise—to tax directly what it wants, as it wants?

REAGAN: Well, I think this is—this is one of the great problems confronting the states today, and indeed endangering the very federal system of—the system of a federation of sovereign states. The federal government has pre-empted so much of the tax source, the state finds itself hard put to find sources without upsetting the economic balance that can keep our economy moving. And then in turn, the state, in its desperation for money, reduces the local community, where the real basic services that people must depend on every day are furnished. Education, police protection, the maintenance of their streets, sewage, garbage disposal, all of these services. And your local communities are even more desperate than the state.

So your states wind up taxing and then by subvention putting a great proportion of the money that is taxed by the State of California back to the local communities.

We go to Washington, and we are faced with this hat-in-hand prospect of asking for federal grants. And I know I'm accused of oversimplifying, but it doesn't make sense to me for the federal government to take that money first, and then dispense it back to you in grants in which they tell you how to spend it from Washington, D.C.

And of course, like an agent for a Hollywood actor, there's a certain carrying charge that's deducted in Washington before you get it back again.

Well, I helped write a resolution for the Republican Governors Conference in Colorado Springs several months ago with a proposal as an experiment that I thought would work—and it *would* work, and might lead away from this federal grant thing. My proposal was that the federal government, as a kind of experiment, designate a percentage—let's say it was only 2 percent of the federal income tax—and as the money is collected in each state, let the Internal Revenue collector for that state send—when he gets the total amount—send 98 per cent to Washington and simply send 2 percent of the total amount to the state government.

This struck me as very plausible, but I raised the question of the common assumption that the federal government needed to engage in some redistributionism between states that needed extra money, and states that were especially opulent.

REAGAN: Yes. This also came up at the Governors Conference. There were governors who said there were states that had to depend, that were poverty states, that didn't have the resources of the big industrial states. I challenge—I question this really. But at the same time, their idea was that if we did this system, and this became effective, then these states would not be getting an additional subsidy.

Now it makes it a little more respectable for those states to get it from the federal government as a federal grant than it does for them to have to admit that what they are saying is, We want our fellow states around us to kick in and help support us. So I made another suggestion then. I said, Well, if this should be true, then wouldn't the first step— Maybe eventually you'd have to discover there is a state that requires a subsidy, requires its fellow men in the country to help it out. But before you come to that, why shouldn't you take those states of lesser income, and if the percentage of income tax is 2 percent for the rest of us, all right, give them a bigger share of their own money back. Let them keep 4 percent, 5 percent, whatever is needed, so that it is their own money being left at home to take care of them, before you have to branch out and see if someone else must take care of it.

I moved on to a problem that I had addressed in my own mayoral campaign two years before: generous welfare payments without a residency requirement:

BUCKLEY: But it [the residency requirement] is a legitimate means, isn't it, of trying to discourage thoughtless traffic among the states? I know that for instance in New York, a commission recommended to Governor Rockefeller a couple of years ago that he institute a residency requirement, incidentally a proposal that he did not proceed to accept. But their reasoning was that if you had a one-year residency requirement, people wouldn't leave a place where they actually have houses and jobs and so on and so forth, simply because of the lure of the emerald city of New York, and then arrive there and immediately become public charges.

But that isn't one of your problems in California?

REAGAN: Oh yes. There's a very—I think even a greater problem. I think this is true of any of the states, Florida, Arizona, California. I think when the wind begins to blow in Minnesota and Michigan, there are many people that if they are free to travel and not lose their welfare checks are going to decide they'd rather be on welfare in California or Florida . . .

BUCKLEY: Yeah.

REAGAN: . . . or Arizona than they would in those colder states.

BUCKLEY: Sure.

REAGAN: And we think that this has been one of our problems, because California, with its great influx of people, continues to have a higher unemployment rate than the rest—than the national average.

BUCKLEY: For that reason, presumably.

REAGAN: Well, I think there's reason to suspect that, because at the same time our welfare burden has been increasing here about four times as fast as the increase in population.

We covered a lot of ground in that televised hour—the principle of federalism; the usurpations of the Supreme Court—before Governor Reagan finished with one of those buoyant passages that resonated so strongly with the American people:

BUCKLEY: Well now, what is it about California other perhaps than the unique contribution of Governor Brown that caused this appetite for reform? Why hasn't it swept other states of the union, for instance?

REAGAN: Well, maybe I have to quote Mark Twain. A hundred years ago Mark Twain was writing about California and he said, "Californians are a different breed." He said, "The easy and the slothful, the lazy, stayed home." And he said, "Californians have a way of dreaming up vast projects and then carrying them out with dash and daring."

BUCKLEY: Even if they are negative.

*(Laughter.)*

BUCKLEY: Well, Mark Twain was a shrewd observer, but do you think that these generous and romantic impulses will one day reach us lazy and slothful at the other end of the . . . ?

*(Laughter.)*

REAGAN: I don't think—I think the pioneer quality is in all America. I think what really happened was simply we perhaps came to the turning point first; I think the fact that we were the highest tax-paying state per capita, that our property tax was almost double the per capita property tax of the country, I think it just simply—the timing was right, that it started here; and when it was presented to the people, the idea of running their own affairs, they grabbed at it and they're, as I say, they're proving that it will work, that the people are interested in government; there isn't an apathy.

For every problem, there are ten people waiting to volunteer if someone will give them a lead and show them where they can be useful.

# 4

Capote and the Reagans

In 1966, Truman Capote gave his party, the Black and White Ball, designed to wipe all other parties from memory. Capote was a fine writer, but was in later years fatally diverted. The first enemy was a combination of booze and dope; the second, indiscretion in his full-time pursuit of glamour and beautiful people.

My wife and I had attended the party. Oglers of all sorts speculated on who had been invited, who had not: some of those who hadn't made the list found it socially necessary to absent themselves from New York altogether on the appointed day, even going to such lengths as traveling to Europe. That way, it might not be discovered that they had not been invited. But Truman ruined that dodge by publishing, the day before the affair, a list of those upon whom he had in fact conferred his Olympian honors.

Though Capote was visibly transported by social noise, he got word to me a few months later that he wanted to talk about a serious project, and I made an appointment to see him.

Truman wanted to make a "definitive" study of capital punishment. He had been greatly moved by his experience with the killers in Holcomb, Kansas, the central figures in his smashing *In Cold Blood*. That book is an engrossing account of what happened after Truman resolved one day in 1959, after reading a *New York Times* account of the event, to investigate the killing of father, mother, son, and daughter in a farmhouse in western Kansas. Capote never really explained what it was that uniquely attracted his attention and, for a considerable time, entirely absorbed his life.

There were two culprits, ex-cons, amateurs, hayseed killers. It was late at night, there was booze and a reported stash of money, and fright. They were picked up a few weeks later, and Truman's petition to interview them was granted. The lead agent of the Kansas Bureau of Investigation was not unmindful of the pleasures to be had from serving as center of attention for this imaginative crime writer. Capote's progressive involvement in the story added to its news value. Six years later, Capote had written his book, *In Cold Blood*, the whole of it published in *The New Yorker*, and the rest is history, on up to an Academy Award–winning movie, *Capote*, in 2005.

It sometimes happens that a death sentence is actually carried out. The death sentences given to Perry Smith and Dick Hickock were quite seriously intended, surviving five years of appeals. And although the storm for an end to capital punishment had begun, it had not yet conquered Kansas, where the breathtaking killings in cold blood had impassioned the justice-keepers. On the other side, dogged watchers of the drama, and they were considerable, were attempting to stop the executions.

These watchers were mostly New York society and literary lions. What if, at the last moment, Marie-Antoinette had escaped the guillotine? It was here and there argued that Truman Capote, having made the two killers national figures, had now been downright sluggish in cooperating with a last-minute legal maneuver that might have delayed the executions, or even quashed the verdict. And then the entire story was electrified by the depths of Truman's attachment to Perry Smith, which had turned the corner into romance.

What Truman had on his mind in 1967, as he told me when we met to discuss it, was a great big TV documentary on capital punishment. He told me he had arranged to inspect most of the country's death houses but had failed in Arizona and in California.

"Ronald Reagan's been governor only a few months, but he is pretty set in his ways, I've found out, and he says nobody—zero, *nobody*—is going to get into '*my* death house.'" Capote laughed his trademark epicene laugh over Reagan's way of referring to the death house. "Some of us don't even *have* a personal death house!"

"And that's where I come in?" I said, somewhat warily.

"That's where you come in, Bill. As an act of piety to art and friendship to your old friend Truman Capote."

Well, it worked. I *was* in fact a close friend of the Reagans, and they had no reason to imagine that I would cooperate in any abolitionist movement in regard to the death penalty.

But a visit to the Reagans by Truman Capote required . . . orchestration. I warned them at dinner that Truman was exhibitionistically gay but that although capable of long stretches of superciliousness, he was nonetheless a man of substance with genuine concern on the whole subject of capital punishment.

Two sequels came hard on the heels of this meeting. Truman was admitted to Governor Reagan's office. Coincidentally, a week earlier, an important aide of Reagan's had resigned abruptly after word reached Sacramento of an overnight scene in a mountain cabin that was manifestly a gay outing.

On the phone after meeting Capote, Reagan told me he was willing to grant Capote's plea to visit the prison. Only much later was I told, and not by Reagan, that after Capote had left the building the governor went out into the hallway and called out: "Somebody call that feller back and troll him up and down a couple of times in case there's anybody else left around here."

TV executives found Capote's documentary, *Death Row U.S.A.*, too grim, and it was never broadcast, though *Esquire* published his essay by the same name. But what did grow out of all this was an absolute bewitchment. The Reagans genuinely fell for Truman Capote, who for his part professed a huge attraction to them. Some months later in New York we had a dinner party for the Reagans. Truman Capote was there and warned me before dinner that he intended to conclude the evening with an elaborate toast with "a wham-bang narrative, Bill, you'll see." And after dessert, it came.

"I was right up to the end of the line of death houses to visit," he said, leaning on the back of his chair, his glass in hand, "and now there was only Arizona. Governor Williams was another friend of our host, and Bill placed a phone call to him just as he'd done to our guest of honor. Williams also agreed to meet with me, but what he said was, 'Mr. Capote, you can go up to the Arizona State Penitentiary, but the warden who runs that place won't take any suggestions from me very kindly, so you'll have to persuade him yourself to let you interview and film the death-house people.'"

Truman let the suspense mount among the twenty guests. "Now wait a minute, wait a minute. The warden wasn't very receptive to my idea of the special documentary. But I was still trying to persuade him, and while I was talking we hear this god-awful noise from the jail corridor outside. And then we saw a guard chasing a prisoner! The prisoner hurls himself down the staircase near where we are sitting, and the guard was holding out his pistol, taking aim. Just when the prisoner reached the bottom of the stairs, the guard shot, and the prisoner fell dead!"

Truman was pleased by the reaction of the guests, though he avoided the eyes of Ronald Reagan. What he got was one part horror, one part sheer amusement, a combination Truman liked.

Those were the glory days. I was immensely saddened the last time I saw Truman Capote. He was acting a part in a movie in which illustrious Hollywood figures, including my friend David Niven, had tiny roles. But at lunch he sat alone. He had committed a final, and quite dispositive, social error. He had sold *Esquire* four chapters of his unfinished novel *Answered Prayers*, which contained gossamer-thinly disguised portraits of various New York social deities, including his erstwhile closest friend,

Babe Paley, wife of CBS magnate Bill Paley, both of whom were, at this point, very erstwhile friends of Truman's. In retaliation, his traduced friends brought down the whole curtain. After 1976, Truman could not have gotten anybody at all in New York to go to a ball given by him. He lived on for another eight years.

# Correspondence, 1967

July 13, 1967

Dear Bill--

It was so good to see you again--I think they should move L.A. closer to N.Y. or something--but it did make for a perfect birthday to have you celebrate it with me, and thank you and Chris again for my present. I'm sorry you couldn't make the party Saturday--it was very posh and lovely! . . .

I loved your BIG SECRET re: Mr. Vaughn[1]--now I have one for you. I think my daughter has a slight crush on you. You may become "the older man" in her life-- after all, every girl should have one, and if she has the good taste to choose you, I'll forgive her remark about the square musicians. Seriously, if she's asked me once, she's asked me ten times when you were coming out again, if we saw you at the Bloomingdales' to be sure and say hello, etc. etc.-- now she's asked if she could send you some of her poetry, as she'd like your opinion on it! . . .

I think you and Ronnie will be at the Bohemian Grove on the same weekend, which should be interesting. We go to the Palisades on the 28th for a month. I can't wait.

---

1. WFB had told Mrs. Reagan that his son was more impressed by the Man from U.N.C.L.E., with whom he did a *Firing Line* on July 8, than by the new governor of California.

Come West again soon--Patti and I will be waiting.

                              XX
                              Nancy
Best to Christopher--


            ✒          ✒          ✒


                              August 30, 1967
Cherie:

A telegraphic communication, pending something
longer later. I didn't answer your letter when it
came because I was up to my ears in the piece on your
estimable husband. Message Center[1] reports that you
received my communication, namely that it was
accepted by *West* magazine. I had hoped they would
turn it down so that we could have a jolly scene, and
I could get it published in a national magazine.
However, they seem rather enthusiastic about it and
will feature it in their October 8 issue. *National
Review* will publish it separately a few weeks later.
It is cagily executed and purposely critical here
and there in order to increase its effect. I have
tried it out on a couple of Reagan fans and was
pleased by their reaction.

Message Center also informs me that Guv was very
obliging on the matter of seeing Truman Capote in
connection with the television special on capital
punishment. I have a piece on Capote's ball in
the December issue of *Esquire*. Will send it to

---

2. WFB's sister-in-law Bill Finucane.

you anon. Capote is an influential guy and worth giving a little time to. Message Center did not, however, report whether Miss Patti had received my comments on her truly talented poetry. Said commentary was sent to Pacific Palisades, so perhaps it accumulated dust there while you were beaching.

I am scheduled to see the preview of Warren Steibel's television series on you next week, and if I find anything there undesirable--which I doubt--I will simply walk up to the camera with big shears and snip it out. Will report either to you or to Message Center my reactions.

Are we then to have the pleasure of giving you that dinner? I do hope so and, subject to your confirmation, have held the evening of December 4. Let me know if there is anyone besides Jackie[2] whom you'd like to have invited. That's all that's urgent at the moment.

Pots of love, as ever,

Bill

Ꮶ     Ꮶ     Ꮶ

September 21, 1967

Dear Nancy:

Got a phone call from Capote, who tells me how wonderfully kind you and Guv were, and how

---

3. Still Kennedy, though soon to become Onassis.

completely you both won him and Mrs. Gimbel[3] over.
They went on and on about your kindness,
intelligence, and hospitality. Thought you'd like
to know. Tell Message Center New York is very high on
you these days.

And yes, as I told MC, January 17 is fine. Let me
know when you feel like it if there is anyone special
you'd like to see. . . . Why hasn't Miss Patti sent me
any more poems?

> As ever,
> Bill

❧        ❧        ❧

> September 27, 1967

Cherie:

John Chafee and his wife have accepted an
invitation to be at your dinner. You will find them
both absolutely charming. Will be fun if we can
disengage him from Romney[4]--perhaps we can brainwash
him. . . . Mrs. Richard Clurman, who will be one of
the guests, is married to the head of correspondents
of Time Inc. They are both old friends of ours. They
are both good fun, and influential. Mrs. Clurman
approached Pat wondering whether we would consider
inviting Governor and Mrs. Nelson Rockefeller! I

---

4. Mary "Piedy" Gimbel, a former United Artists employee, was helping
Capote with the documentary.

5. Liberal Republican presidential candidate George Romney had
explained his changing his mind on the Vietnam War by claiming that when
he visited Vietnam, the U.S. military had brainwashed him.

haven't had time to assimilate that one. But maybe you and Message Center should discuss this and let me have your directive!

> Hastily, and pots of love,
> Bill

❦    ❦    ❦

> November 8, 1967

Dear Patti:

I may be crazy, but I think your poems are terrific, even by the highest standards. You have a controlled rhythm which builds up with enormous force and as in, for instance, your "into the fiery sphere," comes to a wonderful climax in the last three lines. I am going to check my judgment out with Professor Hugh Kenner, the poetry critic, whose book I will send you.

One tiny little mechanical suggestion: when you type poetry, it must be absolutely, totally accurate--no misspellings, mispunctuation, that kind of thing. So watch that. A trivial observation, but having gone as far as you have, you mustn't let down on the minor matters. Keep the poems coming.

Christopher sends his heartiest greetings.

> Yours cordially,
> WFB

# 5

# Is Reagan Running?

Bill Rusher, the publisher of *National Review* and my close friend, followed attentively the vicissitudes of the select (very) few public figures of whom he approved. From the earliest days, before even his election as governor of California, Ronald Reagan made it onto that select list.

Rusher, a graduate of Princeton and of the Harvard Law School, was a political companion of F. Clifton White, a deeply adroit freelance political manager and entrepreneur who operated mainly in New York. He was the unrivaled chief of political intelligence. In 1964, he had labored to nominate Barry Goldwater for president. He did that, but was passed over as campaign manager. Insiders did not question that White's absence from the scene was one reason for Johnson's lopsided victory.

As for Bill, he was as staunch as Mt. Rushmore. His fascination with politics had led him into the core contest in New York, which was between the softs and the hards in the Republican Party. Eventually the hards decided that the only way to make headway against the softs, led in the early 1960s by Nelson Rockefeller, was to apply pressure from the outside. J. Daniel Mahoney and Kieran O'Doherty duly founded the New York Conservative Party, with whose blessing I ran for mayor of New York in 1965, and which would achieve its great victory in 1970, electing my brother James Buckley to the United States Senate.

For three decades, at our fortnightly editorial conferences at *National Review*, we had the opening summary of the publisher, in which Rusher edged forward his *mise-en-scène* of the political world. Early in 1968, he was giving us, week after week, reasons why not Richard Nixon but Ronald Reagan was going to be nominated for president at the convention in Miami in August.

After a few weeks, I thought it time for a showdown. "Bill, we take as a postulate that Reagan is the favorite potential candidate of all of us sitting here, but of course that has nothing to do with how we analyze the scene. Richard Nixon is in fine shape with the GOP. Doesn't he have claims to being treated as heir apparent?"

I thought back on Nixon's appearance on *Firing Line* a few months earlier. It had been followed by dinner at my apartment with two old friends and collaborators.

Two things, completely divergent, stayed in the memory. The first is that, although the *Firing Line* taping was held up for three hours by defective studio equipment, Nixon waited, uncomplaining. All efforts to appease him with food and drink were rejected. "Thanks," he said, shaking his head after the third attempt. "I don't drink when I have to speak." He would have nothing but iced tea. But later, returned back from the studio, he accepted a sherry, I think it was, and talked comfortably into the evening.

Of course, we taxed him about his campaign for the nomination. I remember asking whether he intended to compete in Indiana, where there had been commotion by warring political factions. Yes, he said, he did, and was sure he would win it.

"You're certainly confident in these matters," I observed, without reproach.

"I have never lost a primary."

The information was stunning. "Except," he corrected himself, "to Nelson Rockefeller in 1964 in Oregon." (Nixon was not campaigning in 1964, but he could not prevent the Oregon Republican Party from putting his name on the ballot.)

Even reminded of the record, Rusher would not give way. He foresaw a Rockefeller delegation powerful enough, in Miami, to block a first-ballot sweep by Nixon. "After a couple of Rockefeller-Nixon ballots, the convention will turn to Ronald Reagan."

I reminded Rusher that Clif White, whose political knowledge Rusher traditionally deferred to, was backing Nixon.

"I know. That was a setback. And there was a worse one."

I was curious.

"Strom Thurmond announced yesterday that he was for Nixon."

Thurmond, the senior southern conservative and power broker—surely that settled the question of the Miami convention?

❧      ❧      ❧

It did not help Rusher's cause that Reagan himself was not actively campaigning for the nomination. A group of leading California Republicans had persuaded him to let them place his name on the primary ballot as a favorite son. Their point was to avoid a bruising primary contest among Nixon, Rockefeller, and Romney. That, they convinced Reagan, would only hurt the Republican Party and help the Democrats. So Reagan was on the ballot, but he continued to speak of himself as not a real candidate, while needing to avoid saying or doing anything that would truly have disqualified him from attention. Those who stuck by him undeviatingly, like Rusher, assumed that he would be wafted to power on the strength of his successes in California and his immense popularity with the conservative faithful.

In August, in Miami, a movement for Reagan was distinct. A number of delegates in addition to the California ones pledged their support for Reagan, and his name was actually put in nomination. Notwithstanding that he was not an official candidate, his votes on the first ballot came in at 182. Nixon had 692 (667 were needed to win the nomination), Rockefeller, 277. Reagan dashed to the platform and asked for permission to speak, which the chairman granted after a few minutes of clinging to a procedural rule. Reagan gave an ecumenical oration, appealing for party unity and urging the delegates to nominate Nixon by acclamation. This they didn't do, but all but a handful switched their votes to Nixon.

I filed a column and then left Miami with my wife and several friends aboard my sailing schooner, *Cyrano*, destination Cozumel. At the wharf by the Coast Guard station we completed the necessary preparations for the short ocean passage; we had weighed anchor and were on our way when a bullhorn summons beckoned: "THIS IS A CALL FOR WILLIAM BUCKLEY. YOU ARE TO RETURN TO THE COAST GUARD STATION IMMEDIATELY." I found this disturbing, to say the least. I assumed there was arresting word awaiting me about the health of a member of my family, this being generally how news of this kind reached one offshore in the pre–cell-phone era.

I nosed the bow of the boat up to the pier, gave the wheel to a companion, and bounded up to the station. A Coast Guard officer greeted me, a slip of paper in hand. He directed me to the public telephone booth and gave me the number I was to dial. At the other end of the line was—Ronald Reagan.

His purpose was to compliment me, and to thank me, for the column, which he had just read. "You have it *exactly* right, what I did, why I did it, what I expected."

I had written that Reagan was not a genuine candidate, that he had permitted the use of his name on the floor only to satisfy GOP conservatives, that he was a willing participant in the political exercises ahead aimed at electing Nixon. I had closed my column with a tribute to Reagan, for which he professed gratitude:

He is a man expansively generous, considerate; and it must be both (a) that he never considered, at least not after Nixon's primary victories, the possibility that he would beat Nixon; and (b) that he nevertheless shrank from overruling his idealistic, devoted, and optimistic coterie, who asked him to suspend thought, and dream; dreaming being the substance of the whole elating caper.

It is seldom recognized in politics, in particular where presidential candidates are involved, that gentle and obliging and self-effacing men are capable of inserting themselves into presidential races. Ronald Reagan was one such.

## *Correspondence, 1968–1969*

Dear Nancy:

  Am off tomorrow for Switzerland. Am truly
exhausted. Don't forget, we are to meet at Sammy's
Bar in Casablanca at 11:45 pm on February 17. Travel
lightly, and don't leave a forwarding address.

                      Lots of love,
                      Bill


                ⤸        ⤸        ⤸


                      July 8, 1968
Sweet Nancy:

  How I missed you on your-birthday-my-anniversary.
I thought of that fun visit exactly a year ago. Pat
says you are in splendid shape, but how can you be in
splendid shape so long separated from Your Lover?
Tell Message Center we miss her too, and can't wait
to see you in Miami. I enclose my most recent blow
for Liberty.[1]

                      Love,
                      Bill

---

1. See appendix, p. 243, "Recall Reagan?"

᠍ᡃ         ᠍ᡃ         ᠍ᡃ

August 13, 1968

Dearest Nancy:

The little visit with you was the high point of the
Convention for me. Circumstances were hectic, but I
instantly understood when you sighed that in 36
hours it would all be over . . . What you need is a
good rest--not that you look as though you did:
everyone agreed that you never looked better. If
it's true, then I shall simply have to run for
President of Morocco. Pots of love, in which Pat
joins.

As ever,
Bill

᠍ᡃ         ᠍ᡃ         ᠍ᡃ

August 21, 1968

Bill, dear--

I have *so* much to tell you--aren't you ever coming
out here? Do you have to go to Chicago with Mr.
Vidal?[2] If so, I hope you take your bulletproof vest.
Patti watched you and Mr. Vidal and thought you were
sensational--but my, you should hear her on the
subject of G. V. . . .

---

2. ABC had hired WFB and far-left novelist Gore Vidal to comment on
both parties' national conventions. It was at the upcoming Chicago
convention that Buckley and Vidal would have their famous altercation.

Try to come West--and if you run for President of Morocco, I'll be there.

> Lots of love,
> Nancy

                      ✒        ✒        ✒

> August 27, 1968

Dear Nancy:

What a sweet letter. You're oh so thoughtful. And I was so grateful to Ron for his call. I had indeed hoped that the column would help, and am enraged at your telling me that he didn't see it in the *Los Angeles Times*. I shall make inquiries. I hope to be in California in November--I have to receive an award of sorts from the University of Southern California, and if I may, I'll pop up and say hello. What I wish is that we could all get away for a day or so, but somehow that always seems impossible. I have a really beautiful boat, and if you and Ron can sneak away to the Bahamas at any point this winter, I think you'd enjoy yourselves. . . .

I am on an airplane flying to New York to attempt to persuade the relevant figure to permit the name of Nixon to appear on the Conservative line in New York. It could make an enormous difference. Back this afternoon to Chicago to argue with Vidal. Give my love to Message Center, whom I have neglected, and pots to yourself.

> As ever,
> Bill

🦎     🦎     🦎

November 20, 1968

Dear Nancy:

What fun it was! Granted I resented all those
people who kept distracting us--one of them is
reputed to be the Governor of California. Come soon.

Lots of love,
Bill

P.S. How young Patti has grown up. She is going to be
beautiful like her mother. She already has that fine
expression in her eyes and the grace and wit. Not
bad, not bad at all.

🦎     🦎     🦎

September 10, 1969

Dear Sweet Nancy:

How I have neglected you! (And vice versa.) I do
want you to know, however belatedly, that I thought
of you on the 6th of July. I was traveling en route
to Vienna. Incidentally, henceforth, you need not
refer to me as "Mr. Buckley," but as "Commissioner
Buckley." I was to that high office appointed by our
leader a few months ago, more precisely to the
United States Advisory Commission on Information.
What it means is that I sit down once a month in
Washington with the four other commissioners (the
head of the thing is Frank Stanton of CBS) and we gab
about . . .

And have you spent a pleasant summer? I understand
all goes moderately well with you from Bill
Finucane, and of course I know that Guv is doing
splendidly from all reports. Now the big question:
are you coming soon to see us? If not, I'll simply
have to go to Sacramento.

> Pots of love,
> Bill

ᐟ           ᐟ           ᐟ

> September 26, 1969

Dear Bill,

I thought you had dropped out of my life
completely! I won't mention the months and months
you've neglected me terribly and the awful effect
this can have on a girl--no, I'll be big about it and
we'll proceed as if nothing ever happened--but deep
down inside--ouch.

> Love and Xs,
> Nancy

# 6

# Nixon to China

On July 15, 1971, President Nixon helicoptered from his Western White House in San Clemente to a television studio in Burbank to make a surprise announcement: not only were we ending our ostracism of Red China, but he would himself visit China sometime before the following spring. The shock waves were everywhere palpable; but Mr. Nixon knew enough about politics to know that he might safely proceed from the television studio to a fancy restaurant in Los Angeles, there to celebrate his diplomatic triumph in a highly publicized private dinner at which the champagne corks popped in complacent harmony with the impending public elation. A few precautions were taken, as if by a master electrician running his eyes over the control panel.

I sat viewing Mr. Nixon's television performance as a guest in the Reagans' relaxedly hushed living room in Sacramento, with my brother Jim. Earlier that day, in San Francisco, I had taped two *Firing Lines*, one with the newly elected senator from New York, the other with the newly re-elected governor of California.[1] The coincidence was happy—we conservatives could reflect now together on the meaning of Mr. Nixon's démarche, without pressure.

The governor turned off the television after the network commentators began transmitting the delighted stupefaction of the international diplomatic community. There had been no comment in the room, save one or two of those wolfish whistles one hears when someone on one's side in politics says something daringly risqué; kinky, even, gauged by the standards of the old Nixon. The television off, there was silence in the room for a second, not more—the telephone's ring reached us. The butler appeared. "Dr. Kissinger is on the line," he said to Governor Reagan, who stood up and went to the sequestered alcove where the telephone sat. He wasn't gone for very long, but even by the time he returned, somehow we knew that the question *Did Richard Nixon say something he shouldn't have said? Did he undertake a course of action he should not have undertaken?* was not up for review. The defloration was final. Henry Kissinger, within five minutes of the public announcement, had reached and reassured the most conspicuously conservative governor in the Union that the strategic intentions of the president were in total harmony with the concerns of the conservative community.

---

1. The first was called "The Problems of a Conservative Legislator"; the second, "On Being a Good Governor."

The balance of the evening was given over only glancingly to the great catharsis, which not many months later, by compound interest, would emerge as a Long March jointly undertaken by the United States of America and the People's Republic of China. As I wrote at the time, "The doubters were much more than helpless; they were paralyzed. In a matter of hours the political emotions of the country had been permanently rearranged. To be sure, a few of us lisped out our reservations. My brother, Senator Buckley, issued his cautionary notes. I broke wind with heavy philosophical reservations. But it was much too late. The Zeitgeist was so far ahead of us it had time to stop and laugh as we puffed our way up the steepening mountain. And soon the great day came when, glass raised high in Peking, the President of the United States toasted the Chairman of the People's Republic of China; after which we doubters disappeared from sight."

# *Correspondence, 1972–1976*

Dictated in Hawaii
Transcribed in New York
January 12, 1972

Dear Ron:

You did wonderfully today,[1] and I am pleased among other things that the reservations you expressed last night were not ratified. I think the program was truly useful, and I have to report to you Milton Friedman's total enthusiasm for what you said, how you said it, and the whole of your position. Anyway, my congratulations.

I am taking the liberty of enclosing a copy of a letter I received from an old friend. Normally I wouldn't do this kind of thing, but I think you can see from the quality of that letter, the quality of the person who wrote it. He is a gentleman, a scholar, a friend, and a man of honor. He and I graduated together at Yale. I write to endorse most formally, most emphatically, his nomination to the

---

1. In a *Firing Line* special titled "Conservatives Confront 1972." The other participants were Clare Boothe Luce, Jim Buckley, Representative John Ashbrook (who had just launched a primary challenge from the right against President Nixon), Dan Mahoney (co-founder of the New York Conservative Party), and Milton Friedman.

Superior Court in San Bernardino. I am certain that
if you will read his letter through, you will see
something of the special quality of Joe Campbell. Do
what you can.

Tell Nancy that I have recently heard a disturbing
rumor about her. An informed friend told me he has
reason to believe that she is a secret agent of Mao
Tse-tung. I of course denied this, but I would feel
better about it if she would write me and tell me it
really isn't so.

> As always, your friend,
> Bill

P.S. Interested to learn that they didn't run my
column about you in the *Los Angeles Times*.[2] I find it
especially disturbing because along the way there we
had come to the conclusion that the bad guy was N.W.[3]
Now he is retired, and it continues to happen. Do we
conclude that the entire organization is mobilized
to keep pro-Reagan copy away?

🙚  🙚  🙚

> January 26, 1972

Dear Bill:

Just a line to tell you, first of all, that Nancy is
horrified that her cover has been broken and her
status as a secret agent is at last revealed. She

---

2. See appendix, p. 245, "Reagan and Nixon."
3. Nick Williams, editor of the *Times* from 1958 to 1971, was proud of
having changed the paper's "conservative" image.

intends to disappear and return as a fat blonde sometime in the future, under a different name, of course.

I appreciate your bragging about the program and your kind words.

I was also most interested to read the enclosed letter from that Beverly Hills lawyer. Somehow I don't remember it that way.[4] He overlooks the fact that that conversation, "informal," as he put it, with a group of children, appeared over and over again on T.V. as a sixty-second spot ad in which he held a conversation with one small Negro girl. But then, that's probably the type of thing a fellow would forget.

I've passed on the word to Ned Hutchinson about your friend, and we're glad to have the input. Again, thanks.

Best regards,
Ron

Dictated in Switzerland
Transcribed in New York
March 13, 1972

Dear Ron:

I appreciate the hour I spent with you on the telephone the other night. I have since seen the rather alarmingly complacent statement of Barry

4. The reference is to the ad for Governor Brown in the 1966 campaign of which the punch line was, "An actor shot Lincoln."

Goldwater, to which I am constrained to reply a wee
bit reproachfully. I shall send you a copy as soon as
it is written.[5] I continue to fear for the dissipation
of the anti-Communist reserve. It is very nearly
gone, and I do not know what bloody event will be
necessary to regenerate it.

My friend, might I ask a personal favor? You know
René Wormser, who dined with us the night we heard
the China broadcast. He is a venerable man, of 70
years. He wishes to return, retired, to California.
But he is too active to abandon the law altogether.
It is a requirement, formally, to take the bar exam,
as described in his covering note. It would be an
arduous imposition on someone of his age, and
something of a humiliation for someone of his
distinction. But I am told that there are any number
of precedents, and that the legislature is willing
to oblige. If you would be kind enough to give the
matter to your legal staff, I would be much indebted
to you, as of course would be René Wormser, and Jules
Stein, who is his close friend. I enclose (a) his
letter to me of March 1st, (b) a second letter to me
of March 1st in which he describes his California
background, and (c) his curriculum vitae. I do thank
you.

Pat joins in affectionate greetings to you both.

As ever,
Bill

꙳꙳꙳    ꙳꙳꙳    ꙳꙳꙳

---

5. See appendix, p. 247, "Senator Goldwater's Reassurance."

April 12, 1972

Sweet Nancy:

Tell you what, let's develop a raging controversy
and blast each other in our columns![6] But, for
purposes of chivalry, you go first. On the other
hand, what can you find in me to criticize? Among
other things I have such superb taste in women!

Love,
Bill

᠊᠊     ᠊᠊     ᠊᠊

April 24, 1972

Dear Bill--

But you still haven't told me when you're coming
out here! My peanut butter is getting stale--
Maybe I should answer a question on that--"What
does your favorite columnist, editor, man-about-
town etc. have for breakfast?" That should shake
them up a bit!

XX

᠊᠊     ᠊᠊     ᠊᠊

July 10, 1972

Sweet Nancy:

After neglecting me all these months I am pacified
by your telephone message. I was in the south of

---

6. Mrs. Reagan had started writing a syndicated column, donating the
proceeds to the National League of Families of American POW-MIA.

Turkey, during the last couple of weeks, cruising, and I count it an act of neglect that you didn't offer to scoop me up on Air Force Three or whatever it is you have been traveling in. I sent you a wire to commemorate your birthday and hope the White House communications systems will get it through to you. Longing to see you. My schedule the weekend of the Bohemian Grove is horribly choked up. I had hoped to sneak off and have dinner with you on Monday the 24th after my luncheon talk to the World Affairs Council. But it turns out I have to go to Los Angeles to do the television there with Dan Ellsberg. Is there any chance that you will be in the Los Angeles area on the Tuesday? I must go to visit with my mother-in-law in Vancouver, but if you were going to be there on Tuesday night I'd postpone that until Wednesday morning. Advise.

Lots of love,<br>Bill

✒      ✒      ✒

October 24, 1973<br>CONFIDENTIAL

Dear Ron:

It was grand talking to you after so many weeks (months?), though the circumstances were of course sad.[7] As I suggested, the information that reaches

---

7. As the Watergate investigation forged ahead, Vice President Spiro Agnew, who had become a conservative hero during the first Nixon administration, resigned his office after pleading nolo contendere to charges of taking bribes while governor of Maryland. Nixon had tapped the popular

me privately is that Our Leader is in deep trouble,
and that it is altogether possible that he will not
succeed, finally, in extricating himself. I think the
moment has come delicately to insist, in
declamations aimed urbi et orbi, that Congress must
proceed to confirm the Vice President. Just In Case.
Following that, a patient, cautious dissociation
would appear to be prudent. I enclose, as I said I
would, remarks I delivered, sadly, over the corpse
of Ted Agnew ten days ago, and you will see the
spirit and purpose of the enterprise. There is great
need to expose détente, and I hope the dangers of it
will become palpable before the demonstration of its
phoniness becomes too painful. You will need in due
course to take a position here. I heard it said about
you--by a well-wisher--that it will have to be
Rockefeller in 1976 because you "refuse to wrap your
mind around foreign policy." You must prove such
skeptics wrong, and it is not too early to start. You
should have someone on your staff who is trained to
concentrate full time on such matters--let me know
if you desire suggestions. The best pool is the
young men around Scoop Jackson.[8]

Tell Nancy I can discover no information about the
gentleman she proposes to write the piece about you

moderate Republican congressman Gerald Ford to replace Agnew, but Ford
had not yet been confirmed by the Senate. On October 15, 1973, WFB spoke
about Agnew's downfall to the New York Conservative Party's annual dinner;
that speech is reproduced in *Let Us Talk of Many Things*.

8. Even before he toasted Mao Tse-tung and Chou En-lai in Peking,
President Nixon announced that he was going to Moscow for a summit
meeting with Chairman Leonid Brezhnev, as part of a new policy of
"détente" with the Soviet Union. Conservatives were highly skeptical, but the
leading skeptic in the Senate was not a conservative Republican but the
moderate Democrat Henry "Scoop" Jackson from Washington state.

for the *Saturday Evening Post*. Nor do I have a lot of ideas that fit her specifications. Though Charles J. V. Murphy (formerly of *Fortune*) should be considered. Perhaps you saw his splendid piece on the end of Lin Piao in *National Review* this spring. He ghosted the memoirs of the Duke of Windsor. Retired, expensive, conservative but not typed as such.

I will indeed strive to make my plans for January so as to visit with you. Pat joins in affectionate greetings to you both.

As ever,
Bill

✂       ✂       ✂

January 3, 1974

Dear Bill:

Many thanks for sending Nancy and me your new book, *Four Reforms*. We're delighted to have it; however, as usual the fight is already on as to who gets to read it first.

We hope you and your family had as enjoyable a holiday season as we did here in California. Our best to you in the new year, and thanks, again, for remembering us with your book.

Sincerely,
Ron

✂       ✂       ✂

January 25, 1974

Dear Ron:

You were quite saintly to come and face all those tycoons.[9] But as I expected, you charmed them, and had them eating out of your hand. I can only hope that they will be moved to eat advertising in *National Review*! I am sorry that once again we didn't have a chance to exchange any private talk. That will have to be postponed, yet again. My own feeling is that the wheel is turning decisively against our leader. And of course the question is: should one help to accelerate that turn? This one everyone will have to answer for himself. But it is meet that members of the fraternity would keep each other advised. Pat joins in affectionate greetings to you and Nancy--with renewed gratitude.

As ever,
Bill

꙰      ꙰      ꙰

February 6, 1974

Dear Bill:

Just a line to acknowledge your letter and to thank you for the pleasant lunch. I hope the tycoons got the subtle sell and will do their advertising best.

---

9. Governor Reagan had been the featured guest at a luncheon for *National Review* advertisers and potential advertisers at the Buckleys' apartment in New York.

As to the other point in your note, I have just a sneaking instinct that there may have been, with regard to our leader, "overkill." I am watching the horizon for a ripple on the surface. I think it's time to watch a little bit.

Nancy sends her best. Say hello to Pat, although I haven't forgiven her for not coming downstairs, towel and all.

Best regards,
Ron

✒︎     ✒︎     ✒︎

May 16, 1974

Dear Bill:

Bill, the fellow is exactly right. They are circulating petitions to put on the November ballot a unicameral legislature for our state. I must confess my first reaction was why not? It would be simpler and, of course, less expensive. I've had second thoughts and am opposed to it now, but worry that too many people will stop with only their first thought. I believe something very important would go out of our system of checks and balances, even though the Senate is now chosen on a population basis instead of geographically. We still have a great deal of legislation that will make it through one house and not the other, and many times it is just that longer period of time that enables the people to become aware--to make their wants known by the time a bill has reached that second house. I think we would have much hasty legislation if we had the single system.

> Best regards,
> Ron

     ✒     ✒     ✒

> July 29, 1974

Dear Guv and Nancy:

Those were such happy hours. It occurs to me it has been years and years since I had the undiluted pleasure of your company. So much to talk about, so many subjects we touched on, so many we did not. But I got some bearings, and I will confide to you my thoughts as they crystallize. I spent a great deal of time with George Bush and Bryce Harlow at the Camp,[10] as also with Peter Flanigan. They are not optimistic on the particular matter, and both felt that there was a great sea change in public opinion just this last week. I suspect they are correct. Don't make the mistake of hanging in there too long. With renewed thanks and affectionate greetings,

> As ever,
> Bill

---

10. The Bohemian Grove, a club for high-achieving men, with extensive rustic facilities north of San Francisco. The "particular matter" was the likelihood that President Nixon would survive the Watergate investigation. (In fact, he resigned ten days after this letter was written.)

ʞ̃        ʞ̃        ʞ̃

January 29, 1975

Dear Bill:

My apologies for being so long in writing. I can
only plead the ultimate in confusion that
accompanies leaving after eight years. Now, settled
in my own office in Los Angeles, I can start doing
some of the things I should have done a long time
ago.

First, let me mention the article[11] and tell you
how very much I appreciate all of the space in my
favorite magazine. Chuck Hobbs did a good job
historically, but was overly generous in his
personal comments, which I, of course, enjoy in
spite of a twinge of guilt.

Mainly, however, I write to thank you for your most
thoughtful wire on a very particular day. It
brightened the day and made coming home very
special. I thank you, and Nancy thanks you with a
tear in her eye.

Give our best to Pat.

　　　　　　　　Sincerely,
　　　　　　　　Ron

ʞ̃        ʞ̃        ʞ̃

---

11. "How Ronald Reagan Governed California," by Charles D. Hobbs,
in the January 17 issue of *National Review*.

July 28, 1975

Dear Nancy:

It was a wonderful couple of hours and it went in a flash. But we spoke about important things. If I can find a way to say more effectively what is on my mind, I will reduce it to writing and pop off a letter. You were very discreet about your own desires in this august matter.[12] Could this be because your future thoughts, like mine, are only of Casablanca? My affectionate greetings, and tell Guv he is in my thoughts and I will try to be helpful.

As ever,
Bill

August 15, 1975

Dear Bill--

It was so good to see you--as long as it can't be Casablanca I guess the Palisades will have to do! We did talk about important things and if you'll just come out again and *you* & *I* can get in a corner I'll be less discreet about what my thoughts are on the subject--okay?--but hurry up--

XX
Nancy

---

12. The possibility of Reagan's challenging President Ford for the 1976 Republican nomination.

February 12, 1976

Dear Bill:

Thanks very much for the column[13] and for the note of confidence in the closing line. I have been literally quoting the President as an endorser of my plan. I've also illustrated how federal taxes could be shared using the "estate tax," which, since 1926, has ear-marked a percentage for the states--no strings attached. I have even suggested that a percent of the federal income tax could be retained at the state level.

Nancy sends her best (only she used a different word).

Best regards,
Ron

---

13. See appendix, p. 250, "Upstaging Reagan."

# 7

# Reagan vs. Ford

It had been a feverish summer for Ronald Reagan. He had, only a few months before, served out his second term as governor. But a move with great drama had been generated, namely to sidle President Ford off the scene at the White House and let Reagan compete for the presidency in 1976.

Ford was suffering in part because history had cast him in pallid colors, which featurelessness had recommended him to Richard Nixon in the waning days of his presidency. There had been melodramatic interventions: nobody could reasonably have assumed base venality on the part of Spiro Agnew—to do this required more perspicacity than even Nixon had. Nobody could reasonably have predicted the dramaturgy that would result from Agnew's having taken in pocket change from some Maryland contractors years before.

All of this accompanied the scene-by-scene collapse of Richard Nixon, whose successor, Mr. Ford, could not contrive to hold center stage even in his own party. Well, who could?

Reagan. And, of course, Nelson Rockefeller. But now Rockefeller was vice president and judged, by orderly people, as being disqualified to travel from governor to nothing to vice president to president in one incestuous operation.

The problem for Reagan was that he had not made known his own availability before President Ford had (a) announced his intention of running and (b) corralled the support of prominent American conservatives who would have been expected to go with Reagan if he were running. Conspicuous among these were the head of Ford's election committee, Howard "Bo" Callaway, who had run for governor of his home state, Georgia, and lost because he was too conservative; Dean Burch, who had been second in command in the Goldwater campaign in 1964; and David Packard, a Californian who had held a high position in the Defense Department in the Nixon administration.

I pulled my oar that summer of 1975, writing several columns on the subject of Reagan vs. Ford. In one of these I summed up why I believed that, even with Ford's early moves to co-opt conservative backing, Reagan could still prevail. "Reagan's threat to Ford," I wrote,

> is that he was born with an uncanny ability to persuade: to marshal his arguments in a way that combines drama and didacticism. I have, in my extensive experience listening to public speakers, come across only one or two people who are his match. That is the Reagan threat. After putting him on television about the $60-billion deficit, you would see the same

thing happen as when Jonathan Edwards went to Yale and preached—"infidelity skulked, and hid its head."

That is the reason why Mr. Reagan cares less than the professionals think he should care about the matter of announcing quickly, and lining up his political allies quickly. He wants them, of course; but he assumes that they will come to him in due course—if only he proves that he can do to Ford what Eugene McCarthy did to Lyndon Johnson.

Finally, in December 1975, Reagan did announce, and promptly zoomed ahead of Ford in the polls. Leading to the conclusion that whatever else might go wrong in his campaign, there was nothing wrong with his sense of timing.

# 8

## Schweiker for Veep?

I greeted David Keene in my office. "It's important," he had said over the telephone.

Keene was a young but highly experienced figure in the conservative world. I had met him when Young Americans for Freedom was founded, in 1960, in Sharon, Connecticut (at Great Elm, the Buckley family home). He had graduated from the law school at the University of Wisconsin. Soon after the young conservative group was organized, he became its chairman. He went to work then as an assistant to Vice President Agnew and later as an aide to my brother Jim, whom I had dubbed the Sainted Junior Senator from New York. Keene was now—July 1976—Southern Regional Director for the Reagan campaign.

Tall, relaxed, humorous, he came right to the point: "It's got to be Schweiker. Vice president."

"Schweiker?" My curiosity was unfeigned.

"Yes. There's that trouble. Nobody knows him. But he is critical."

Keene explained. In two weeks (August 16) the GOP convention would convene in Kansas City. After stumbling badly in New Hampshire and Florida, Reagan had changed his campaign strategy in North Carolina and won dramatically. But Gerald Ford hadn't folded, and after the last primary vote the two were running neck and neck.

"Governor Reagan is very strong," Keene told me, "but he doesn't have quite enough committed delegates. If we can swing Pennsylvania, we'll make it."

Why was Pennsylvania critical?

"It has a huge chunk of delegates, and there's no primary there, so they're technically uncommitted. Problem is, we hear they're leaning toward Ford. There's only one way to get into that Pennsylvania stronghold, and that's to offer them the vice presidency."

"So, Schweiker?"

"Yes."

"And how am I supposed to generate enthusiasm for Schweiker?"

"You're supposed to be the leading conservative commentator—I'll leave that up to you."

I asked who else had been made aware of the plan.

"You, Roger Milliken, and Strom Thurmond. That's all."

I said I'd have to think about it.

The call came late Sunday afternoon. "What do you think, Bill?"

I told him I had done a little research on Schweiker. "Did you know he registered 89 on the ADA scale?"

In 1947, when the Democratic Party was heavily influenced by the call to nominate Henry Wallace for vice president the following year, as President Harry Truman's running mate, such prime movers as Chester Bowles, Eleanor Roosevelt, Hubert Humphrey, Arthur Schlesinger Jr., and John Kenneth Galbraith reacted by founding the Americans for Democratic Action, a combative left-wing but sturdily anti-Communist political group. The ADA drew up a table of measurements by which to register its approval or disapproval of political figures. To receive a rating of 100 signified an endorsement of every left-oriented measure of the day, such as expanded federal welfare, pro–labor-union legislation, etc. On the ADA scale, Senator Robert Taft would have come in at approximately 5 or 10, Senator Hubert Humphrey at 90 or 100.

I heard a whistle at the other end of the line. Keene dwelled on the figure. "ADA 89." After a pause he said, "He's in favor of capital punishment and prayer in schools, and opposed to abortion and détente."

"Yes," I said. "That's good."

I could hear what I took to be a chuckle at the other end of the line.

"I'll give out the word on Schweiker in the next couple of days. Among other things, I have to talk to *him* about it."

I said that I warranted he would be as surprised as anyone. But that if the gratitude of the Pennsylvania delegation was reliable, nothing else mattered in considering the operation.

I wound up writing four columns on Schweiker over the next two weeks, in the last of them analyzing the ADA rating and going through the list of issues on which Schweiker sounded like one of us. But in the end, the maneuver lost Reagan more conservative delegates than it gained him liberal ones. Pennsylvania went for Ford 93 to 10.

## 9

# Thanksgiving at the Buckleys'

Several published essays on the Reagan children are reproach-ful in the matter of their upbringing. They were neglected, it is commonly said, because of the absorption of their parents in each other. At a couple of points in the narrative I was involved firsthand.

Nancy sent Patti to the Orme School, a boarding school in northern Arizona, which one of my nephews also attended. Patti was in her teens and rigorously pursued the art of poetry. Her letters to me teemed with her love for poetry and her ambition to perfect her skills. I found sadnesses that were striking, and youthful melodrama, but also a pronouncedly live ear (". . . and

THE REAGAN I KNEW

begin again, / walking / a frayed path / on our circular battle-
ground, / finding nothing / that wasn't there before. We are
rooted / in this impasse. / Secure in battle, / we cling / to words /
dripping / caution"). When, at work on this book, I spoke over
the phone of her daughter's poetry, Nancy exclaimed that she
hadn't thought of it for years.

Alongside there is the denial, by no means ambiguous, by
Ron Jr. of any interest in religion. He had concluded—at age
twelve, he told an interviewer a couple of years ago—that the
whole exercise was superstitious and useless. From that age on
he declined to accompany his family to the Sunday religious services to which they often went.

The withdrawal, by Ron Jr., of any interest in spiritual life
illuminates a study of him as well as of his parents. But of
course inquiries into parents' concern for their children's education are quickly arrested by citing individual inclinations to
come up with alembics for one's own philosophical system.
What efforts were made—if any—to acquaint the boy with the
historical and philosophical role of God in history? We do not
need to assume that this would require a familiarity with the
Ninety-Five Theses of Luther or the causes of the Thirty Years'
War. It is popular in quarters of young America to believe that
deference to individual religious inclinations eliminates any risk
of submitting to indoctrination.

When Ron Jr. went on to reject his father's political positions,
ruing the Reagan presidency, it was not necessarily the result of
alienation from the family per se. Weight by the son to his father's principles is here given, here withheld, after thought is paid
to them, cursory or profound, and how they figured in the alle-
giances of the parent.

Ron Jr.'s exposure to family biases could hardly have been more intense. He was eight when his father was elected governor of California, sixteen when his father left office, and eighteen when he was dispatched to Yale for higher education, a few weeks after his father had failed to wrest the nomination away from Gerald Ford.

One weekend, back then, is vivid in the memory. It had been arranged that the Reagans—father, mother, son—would spend Thanksgiving 1976 in Connecticut as guests of the Buckleys. There would be Thanksgiving lunch at Great Elm, in Sharon, and the balance of the weekend as houseguests of me and my wife, Pat, at our home in Stamford, on Long Island Sound. But when the Reagans arrived in Sharon, there was tension.

"Tell Bill about it," said Nancy, drawing her husband and me to one side.

The story was that Ron Jr., in his first semester at Yale, had decided to quit college—more or less immediately. I expressed doubt that he was having academic problems, which indeed he was not, and his parents brought me to the heart of the matter. What moved him was a voracious desire to dance professionally. He wanted to train, beginning immediately, as a ballet student.

Reagan told me that he had frankly given up, on the two-hour drive from New York City, trying to deflect his son from his resolution. In whispers, he and Nancy had conferred on a tactical retreat. Ron Jr. must proceed with his college work until the end of the semester, and only then go off to ballet school, from which he could return to his studies at Yale at any time in the future. Ron Jr. had said no. I was given the assignment of persuading him otherwise.

The rest of the day was dotted with family meetings, the Reagans together, of course, but then various Buckleys with various

Reagans, according as it was hoped that my wife might be especially influential, or my aged mother, or some or all of the half dozen of my brothers and sisters who were there for Thanksgiving. These meetings were interrupted first by the repast, and then by the annual football game, at which, this time around, Ronald Reagan, sometime governor of California, aspirant president of the United States, was elected captain of the A Team and distinguished himself for a half hour, outdone in virtuoso passing and catching only by B Team ingénue Ronald Reagan Jr., about to be ex-Yale 1980.

Individually and in groups—my brother Jim, a Yale graduate, had a round or two—we attempted to make the point that Ron Jr. should give the academic life a better try. He in turn stressed the point that already, at eighteen, he was far behind in studying dance.

"They begin," he explained to me patiently but doggedly, "at age twelve. There's no way I can go back and dance full time from age twelve. But I am really sunk at this point if I set my training back another week." That was his position and he held to it, returning to New Haven only to pick up his baggage, and reporting immediately to a dance school.

The balance of the weekend, in Stamford, was warm, but distracted by the wrench of Ron Jr.'s decision to go it alone.

And Ronald Reagan was as determined to subject his son to poverty as Ron Jr. was to live in it. Ron Jr. was entirely submissive in his sequestration—austerity was a part of his theatrical occupation. He was soon picked up by the Joffrey Ballet, and got performances in its second division.

After a few years he left the ballet and made his way—with his wife, Doria, a psychologist—as a commentator and journalist.

# Correspondence, 1976–1977

Dearest Nancy:

It was swell talking with you and Ron. This is to
confirm that the house, completely staffed but
otherwise empty, is available to you and Ron the
weekend of the first of October. There are four
bedrooms in the main house and a guest bedroom in
Christopher's apartment over the garage. Our driver
and car would be available to you. All you have to do
is call Frances Bronson at my office and tell her if
you are going to use the house. The cook and two
maids will be waiting for you, and you would have
only to instruct them when you want to eat and how
many guests there will be. It would give us great
pleasure to facilitate you in this way, so please
don't hesitate to take advantage of it and to invite
young Ron and his friends to use the house as their
own.

Love,
Bill

January 5, 1977

Dear Ron:

I gave you and Nancy a buzz in Los Angeles, in the mad hectic few hours I was there, but your home didn't answer. I reached the office and learned you were en route to your country place with all those eights in the telephone number, which did not reply. Can I assume that you were picked up in the National Jeep?

It was a splendid visit and I much enjoyed seeing you and Nancy at leisure and spending time with Ron Jr. The more I reflect on the matter, the wiser I think you both are to endure bravely his decision. To oppose it at this point would encourage a bitterness that simply will not occur if you let him make his own way, stressing only the necessity that he acquire a broad musical education as he goes. I would especially enjoin on him a study of harmony. It is an intellectually tough subject, a knowledge of which tends to distinguish proper musicians from such amateurs as myself.

I meant to discuss with you while you were at Wallacks Point the Panamanian issue. I think you didn't see my columns on the subject and under the circumstances I am enclosing them. Let's put it down on the agenda for when we next meet, which I pray will be soon. Pat joins in affectionate greetings to you both.

As ever,
Bill

January 10, 1977

Dear Bill:

Nancy and I are sorry we missed your call when you were out here. We remember and talk much about our weekend with you--as we go about the arduous business of trying to peel off the pounds we both put on.

I still haven't read your columns on Panama because the enclosure in your warm and appreciated letter turned out to be an article (not by you) on the relative safety of airlines. I was glad to get it and to learn that American airlines are two and a half times as safe as the world average. But it didn't even mention Panama--except indirectly, when it said that Central American airlines were four times as dangerous as the world average.

Bill, you also did not enclose a bill (as you promised you would) for one fine life preserver, which arrived in good condition and now hangs on our dock, suitably painted by me. I have discovered a talent for sign painting. Please tell me what I owe.

Nancy sends her love and please give our warmest greetings to Pat.

Sincerely,
Ron


꒒        ꒒        ꒒


January 13, 1977

Dear Ron:

I tried to reach you by telephone but you were out. I write to ask whether you would be kind enough to

sign a letter on behalf of the Conservative Party of
New York. You are familiar with its outstanding
work, having appeared yourself at one of its annual
dinners. As a result of the defeat of Jimmy, it is
temporarily demoralized.[1] Meanwhile the Liberal
Party is riding high, so it is especially important
to have a viable Conservative Party. Nobody in
America is more greatly trusted than you, and I know
that nobody could do the job you could do. I attach a
couple of suggested paragraphs for you to tinker
with as you see fit.

I trust all goes well with Ron Jr. I will give him a
call before leaving on Saturday (for Latin America
and Europe). If you have an extra plot for my new
novel, please send it to me collect. Pat joins me in
affectionate greetings to you and Nancy.

As ever,
Bill

ʡ          ʡ          ʡ

January 26, 1977

Dear Bill:

I'm afraid I have to beg your understanding on the
request to do a letter for the Conservative Party.
May I have a rain check to be cashed at a later date?

---

1. Jim Buckley had been defeated for re-election to the Senate by Daniel
Patrick Moynihan, whose tough-minded performance as UN ambassador had
made him immensely popular.

Here briefly is what has happened. I did a letter for Jesse, a letter for A.C.U.,[2] some letters for some causes and people out here. And, of course, earlier had done some for the congressional committee and the President (you remember him). Well, suddenly we discovered a number of these outfits and individuals had taken the one-time permission to mean perpetuity. People were getting Ronald Reagan letters on a daily basis. I even got some myself.

We've been turning them off as fast as we learn of them, but some damage has been done. In short, right now, I'm not exactly the best bet they could find.

Let everyone get over hearing from me on a daily basis, and at a later date I'll be happy to sign a letter. I know you'll understand. Right now a letter from me could be a kiss of death.

Best regards,

Ron

cc: Mr. Lyn Nofziger

---

2. Senator Jesse Helms of North Carolina had given Reagan very good strategic advice in 1976, leading to the resuscitation of his campaign against Gerald Ford. The American Conservative Union is more or less the conservatives' answer to the liberals' Americans for Democratic Action.

Dictated in Switzerland
Transcribed in New York
February 17, 1977

Dear Ron:

You have a shrewd point about the ultimatum
written into the rhetoric of that awful general.[3]
But isn't it a part of the responsibility of big
nations to transcend provocative jibes from silly
little dictators? I'd have thought so. In any event,
I may write one of these days on the subject. On the
balance of my analysis, I feel pretty secure, and it
reassures me that you tend to agree with me there,
though reaching a different conclusion for the
reasons you gave. Am hard at work on my second novel.
Meanwhile, my sailing book seems to be doing very
nicely, thank you.[4] I trust young Ron is not enjoying
himself too much! Pat joins me in affectionate
greetings to you both.

As ever,
Bill

---

3. Panama, ruled by General Omar Torrijos, was negotiating with the
United States a pair of treaties that would turn over control of the Canal
Zone to Panama immediately, and operation of the canal itself in 2000.

4. *Stained Glass* was the second novel in the Blackford Oakes series.
*Airborne* was an account of WFB's first crossing of the Atlantic as captain of
his own sailboat.

March 8, 1977

Dear Bill:

All the way from Switzerland! If it was snow you wanted, what's wrong with Buffalo?

By now you've probably heard the new rumblings about Mr. Linowitz and the Canal.[5] It seems a number of bankers have a vested interest in draining the canal since Torrijos is a heavy borrower and they're afraid of getting stuck with his bad paper. Among them is Marine Midland, whose loans amount to 128% of total capital. At least that's the charge being made in Congress. I'm waiting to see how much hits the fan, since the charge will be made public later this week.

Nancy sends her best, and give our regards to Pat. Have fun, and wouldn't it be something if a new shenanigan should be forthcoming--this time on the proper side of the fence.

Best regards,
Ron

✒     ✒     ✒

June 8, 1977

Dear Ron:

Am terribly sorry an appointment with three people in Stamford set up two weeks ago prevents me from

---

5. Washington lawyer Sol Linowitz was President Carter's personal representative on the negotiating team. He was also a director of Marine Midland and of Pan Am, both of which had financial interests in Panama. Jesse Helms and others were raising these issues in the Senate.

being with you. I hope you know that nothing would give us greater pleasure than for you to pop out for the evening or for the weekend. My number in New York (679–7330) can put you right through to Stamford, and we can catapult you out in one of the limousines I bought at Jimmy Carter's auction.

On a political matter: pray do not by word or deed permit yourself to endorse the mayoral candidacy of Mr. Goodman.[6] He is indistinguishable from John Lindsay, and can only be supposed to be interested in becoming mayor of New York upon finding a block or two of the city that Lindsay neglected to afflict. My own support is going to Barry Farber, who will compete in the Republican primary and will get the Conservative Party endorsement. As much more on the subject as you desire from

                              Your servant,
                              Bill
bcc: Mr. J. Daniel Mahoney

---

6. State Senator Roy Goodman was, post Rockefeller and Lindsay, the leading liberal Republican in New York State.

# 10

# *Firing Line* and the Panama Canal

M y television program, *Firing Line*, was modestly designed—"No production values!" exclaimed one horrified TV executive—though perhaps immodestly conceived. The
basic idea—it was that of Tom O'Neil, who was chairman of
RKO General—was to have me on the air each week, discussing,
or arguing, one particular subject with one or two guests for an
hour.

RKO Radio Pictures had been a glamorous Hollywood studio,
home of such as Cary Grant, Fred Astaire, Ginger Rogers, and
Katharine Hepburn. It had run into commercial pitfalls in the
fifties and found itself owned by eccentric billionaire Howard

Hughes. Very soon he tired of it, and moved to get rid of what was left of the company—an extensive film library and some real estate in Boston and New York. It was Tom O'Neil who negotiated the purchase with Hughes on behalf of the company founded by his father, the General Tire and Rubber Company. O'Neil had already acquired a number of valuable broadcasting licenses, including WOR radio and TV in New York, and he merged these with his new acquisition under the name RKO General.

O'Neil was a restless political conservative, which is to say one of those conservatives who chide themselves for the platonic character of their attachment. Tom believed all the things generally associated with the conservative movement in the 1960s: —Be tough on Soviet matters, skeptical about their reiterated commitments to peace and order. Look about keenly on the world scene for evidence of Soviet exploitation, and checkmate the Communists whenever possible, using diplomacy, economic intervention, and armed resistance. —Be skeptical of the popular assumption that Franklin D. Roosevelt had the correct formula for judging the state's responsibilities; resist government programs that are inflationary in structure and statist in impact. And —Don't feel you have to laugh at their jokes.

Most conservatives who don't have opportunities to express their differences with liberal commentators—or legislators or teachers or editors—can find passive relief by listening in on, and applauding, the conservative resistance. It was to create such an opportunity by having me enter the fray as a combatant that Tom O'Neil, to the dismay of some of his corporate colleagues, called me to his office in January 1965.

O'Neil was a tall, quiet man, reserved in manner yet of the breed, one quickly got the impression, who are so because they move in circles in which it is unnecessary to be assertive. Control is accepted, by custom, usually when backed by dominant stock ownership.

Tom had an idea. He had been watching when I engaged in a serious spoken brawl with a prominent liberal.

"My idea"—O'Neil spoke in few words—"is to set up thirteen programs [thirteen is the basic cycle in the broadcasting world] featuring, each one, you and a liberal antagonist. You whale away at each other for an hour. And—"

"—and we good people win the war!" I concluded.

He smiled and offered me a drink and said, yes, that was about it. The show would be produced, he said, under the auspices of RKO, with immediate airing over its five home stations, which included WOR in New York City.

We agreed in principle, but then I wound up, in the summer and fall of 1965, running my "paradigmatic" campaign, as I called it, for mayor of New York. So it wasn't until the following year that we could act on O'Neil's idea.

I conferred with the (deputized) producer, and we decided to call the program *Firing Line*. At the end of the contracted thirteen weeks the program was renewed by RKO for another thirteen weeks, and following that, still another. We eventually moved to the Public Broadcasting Service, and carried on for another thirty years. *Firing Line* ended its life, finally, as the longest-running public-affairs program in history featuring the same host, 1966–1999.

I maneuvered very soon to find my own producer and chose Warren Steibel, a self-described political liberal who soon became a close friend and indispensable collaborator. Warren was an enthusiast for *Firing Line*'s regular weekly programs to the end of its life, but he also came up with the idea of doing special two-hour programs four or five times per year, most of them formal debates. The first of these, in January 1978, was a debate on an issue that had divided the American Right.

The issue, the future of the Panama Canal, had become acute when President Carter, succumbing to cries for the Canal Zone to be ceded to Panama, signed a treaty to that effect. This would mean a diminution of American control over the canal itself, and a hint of any such thing—especially so soon after the Vietnam debacle—greatly alarmed conservative America.

I traveled to Panama in the fall of 1976, wrote several columns, and did two conventional *Firing Line* programs. The visit caused me to change my opinion on the proposed Panama Canal Treaty. Departing from conservative ranks, I wrote urging the Senate to ratify the treaty, mainly on the grounds, as I wrote in one of those columns, that Panamanians of all political colorations saw "the reintegration of the Canal Zone as something of a magical restoration of the nation's dignity: the elimination of an ugly birthmark that now condemns Panama to wander around the world conspicuously sullied."

Earlier that year, Governor Ronald Reagan, energetically campaigning for president, had been rallying conservative forces to stand behind existing arrangements. Reagan had lost narrowly in the New Hampshire primary and then again in Florida. But in North Carolina, he thought to make his opposition to the treaty a major part of his campaign—and he won. This propelled a heavy political movement toward him. It proved too late to wrest the nomination from President Ford. But Reagan did not forget the impact, especially among conservatives, of his stand on the Panama Canal.

We went back and forth on the subject over the next year, in public and in private. Then late in 1977 I asked him, in the course of a telephone conversation, whether he would consent to debate the subject in a two-hour *Firing Line*. His first reaction was to say, "Why would *I* want to get into a debate with *you*?" But eventually he reconsidered.

# Correspondence, 1977

Dear Ron:

I know that we are almost certain to continue
disagreeing in the matter of the Canal, but I am most
anxious both to read everything you say on the
matter, and to have you read everything I write on
the matter, and accordingly I am asking Miss Bronson
to send you all the columns I have written on the
subject since the announcement of a month or so ago.
It would be good to talk to you about it, and I'll
look for an opportunity. Sorry you couldn't join me
in New York.

With warm regards,
Bill

September 27, 1977

Dear Bill:

I was happy to get your letter and have read all
your fine columns; however, I must confess that we
are still disagreeing on the matter of the Canal. I

am enclosing some things that I have done, including my testimony before the Senate Committee.

I appreciate your kind words about me in several of the columns and am happy we carry on our disagreement in this manner. I assure you, it could not in any way affect the friendship I feel for you.

I look forward to a day when we can sit down and discuss this, so won't try to argue any of my points in this letter. One thing I do hope you understand is that I have not simply been demanding the status quo. I believe there are alternatives, other things we could do, as you will note in some of the material that I am sending to you. I am concerned about the seeming weakness in which we did not negotiate, we simply made concessions. The United States, dealing from strength, could say to the Panamanians that we are interested in internationalizing the Canal, and possibly creating an American Canal in which the governing board would consist of representatives of all our neighbors in North, Central, and South America.

But this we can discuss, drink in hand, when we have an opportunity.

Again, thanks and best regards.

Sincerely,

Ron

✒        ✒        ✒

October 12, 1977

Dear Ronnie:

Thanks for your good letter. You have some extremely good material, and I think our public discussion of the affair will be extremely lively. I am trying to think offhand of a precedent--two old warriors, united in the faith, differing on a particular. It should be refreshing.

> With warmest regards,
> Bill

ఈ          ఈ          ఈ

December 8, 1977

Dear Ron:

Everybody's been hard at work since your decision to go with the debate, and I think it is shaping up nicely. Mike Deaver will probably have reported a conversation with Warren Steibel, advising you that Sam Ervin will preside, and that four experts, all conservatives, two of them on your side, two (if I can find them!) on my side, will do the questioning. There will also be a period during which we question each other. I hope to arrange to have Sol Linowitz, and perhaps also Admiral Moorer and General Brown,[1] in a so-called experts' panel to answer questions. Boy, I should have gone to Broadway! Tell Ron Jr. if he washes out at his school, he can manage me!

---

1. Admiral Thomas Moorer, a former chairman of the Joint Chiefs of Staff, opposed the treaties, on the grounds that they would help Torrijos and thus help the "Torrijos-Castro-Moscow axis." General George S. Brown, current chairman of the Joint Chiefs, supported the treaties "because we feel they are right."

Will keep you posted. Meanwhile, longing to see you both. It seems to me this is as long a period between visits as any ever, and I resent it.

With warm personal regards,
Bill

# 11

# *Firing Line*: The Debate

The great day came. Some have assigned to this debate something of historical significance. Whether this is to inflate its effect, I do not know. I happen to believe, as I wrote at the time, that Reagan's conspicuous position on the treaty, combined with the treaty's ratification by the Senate, made possible his election as president in 1980. My thesis was (and is) that if he had favored the treaty, he would have lost his hard initial conservative support. But if the treaty had *not* passed the Senate, which it might not have done if the conservative opposition to it had been unanimous, uprisings in Central America during the 1980 presidential campaign might have frustrated Reagan's hopes.

As plans for the debate took shape, we weren't after all able to get Sol Linowitz, but we did even better, getting the principal treaty negotiator, Ambassador Ellsworth Bunker. He would not

THE REAGAN I KNEW

take sides in the debate but would be on hand to answer technical questions concerning the treaty put to him from either side.
And we did get Sam Ervin, recently retired from the Senate,
where he had presided over the liquidation of Richard Nixon. I
suggested to Reagan that each one of us bring along two debating partners and one military expert.

I picked my team, and Reagan picked his.

On my side were my colleague James Burnham, who had
been a senior editor of *National Review* since its inception and
was the foremost (in my judgment) anti-Communist strategist in
the free world, and George Will, who had briefly served as *National Review*'s Washington columnist and had become one of
the nation's premier polemicists, a journalist of high style and
learning. My military expert was Admiral Elmo Zumwalt, former Chief of Naval Operations, and a stalwart and resourceful
anti-Communist.

On Reagan's side were Patrick Buchanan, the talented author, columnist, and polemicist, who had been an able and resourceful assistant to Richard Nixon; and Professor Roger
Fontaine of Georgetown, a highly informed anti-Soviet expert
specializing in Latin America. Reagan's military expert was Admiral John McCain Jr., former CINCPAC (Commander in Chief,
Pacific Command), the (theoretical) supreme commander of our
military forces during much of the Vietnam War, and the father
of future senator and presidential candidate John McCain.

All the participants—except for Fontaine, whom I hadn't
known—were personal friends, many of them current or former
colleagues.

The question before the house: "Resolved, That the Senate
should ratify the proposed Panama Canal treaties."

Reagan was the first speaker. He performed eloquently for fifteen minutes. I followed for fifteen minutes. Each of our seconders made a briefer statement. Then the time came for the cross-examination.

ERVIN: At this time . . . the chair will recognize Governor Reagan and give him the privilege of questioning William Buckley.

REAGAN: Well, Bill, my first question is, Why haven't you already rushed across the room here to tell me that you've seen the light? [*Laughter and applause.*]

BUCKLEY: I'm afraid that if I came any closer to you the force of my illumination would blind you. [*Laughter and applause.*]

REAGAN: Well, all right. The United States has run the Canal at no profit. We have maintained its neutrality throughout the history of the Canal. We have certainly vastly benefited Panama. What do we gain by making this change?

BUCKLEY: Well, what we gain by making this change, to quote myself, is increased security and increased self-esteem. . . .

I called on Ambassador Bunker to speak to a technical question, and then Reagan resumed his interrogation.

REAGAN: Bill, the next question is, If the Canal is so unimportant to us commercially, defense-wise, or whatever, why don't we just *give* it to them? Why do we *pay* them to take it off our hands? And if it *is* important to us, why don't we *keep* it?

BUCKLEY: You have outlined nonexclusive alternatives. In the first place, under the projected treaty there would be a net income to the United States for the next twenty-two years. In the second place, under the projected treaty, there would be a period of orderly transition during which power gradually accumulates in the Panamanian government. I would like to, if I may, supplement my answer to your question by reasserting that there *is* an importance to the Canal, but that its importance is precisely *protected* by that treaty. And let me ask Admiral Zumwalt to give the military reasons why this is so.

ZUMWALT: The military reasons why . . . ?

BUCKLEY: Why it is so that our security is *enhanced* by this treaty.

ZUMWALT: The situation, in thumbnail, is the following. The United States has surrendered strategic nuclear superiority to the Soviet Union. This means that *conventional* military war is likelier. It means that, as both you and Governor Reagan have said, the need for the Panama Canal is *vital*. We *must* be able to deploy ships from one ocean to another in choosing which of our allies we will save, because we can't save them all. The best security—the best certainty—the likeliest probability of being able to use that canal is to have a friendly regime in support of the operation rather than a hostile regime. Those of us who have had to deal with insurgencies—as I did in Vietnam—can tell you that it is impossible to defend that canal, as all the Joint Chiefs have agreed, against a hostile insurgency and that the odds are greatly increased that that insurgency would occur if the United States fails to ratify these treaties.

Then it was my turn to interrogate Reagan:

BUCKLEY: Well, let me ask you to give me the answer to a question which you cannot document, but in which I permit you to consult only your insight. Would you guess that the Panama-

FIRING LINE: THE DEBATE

nian people would prefer, or not prefer, to exercise sovereignty over their own territory? Take as long as you want to answer that. [*Laughter and applause.*]

REAGAN: I was just sitting here wishing that I had with me the transcript of the impassioned plea that was made to United States senators at a meeting of the Civic Council a week or so ago in Panama. The Civic Council is made up of representatives of all the towns in the Canal Zone. The speaker was a black—a Panamanian, not an American. His father, a West Indian, worked on the canal, in building the canal. The speaker had worked all his life on the canal, and his impassioned plea was, even though he was a Panamanian, "Don't! Don't do this! Don't ratify those treaties!"

I could quote the *Chicago Tribune* reporter who did a man-on-the-street thing in Panama with many Panamanians—some refused to give their names, but they answered. But many of them were so outraged that they didn't care. They gave their names even though relatives and friends were pulling at their sleeves and saying, "Don't answer! You'll go to jail!"

BUCKLEY: If what you're saying, Governor, is that Torrijos has *enemies*, it seems to me that you do not need to say that at any length because I concede that he does. Among his enemies are yourself and myself and anybody who has any respect for human freedom. But it is a worldwide phenomenon that irrespective of the ugly character of the ruler, people do desire independence. They do desire sovereignty. There were Russians who fought even under Stalin and fought to the death to defend their territory. Why is it that those impulses which you so liberally recognize as beating in the breasts of people all over the world should suddenly stop beating in Panama because of Torrijos?

REAGAN: Well, I have to ask, Bill, whether this urge is all that strong on the part of the people. As I've said before, we deal with a government that does not represent the will of the people. The people never had a chance to express their will, and—

BUCKLEY: But it was before Torrijos became the dictator that the initial riots took place demanding an assertion of that sovereignty. How do you account for that?

REAGAN: I think the first time that it was expressed was in 1932 in the charter of the new Communist Party of Panama. They put as one of their top objectives the taking over of the canal.

BUCKLEY: Are you saying that the Communists invented patriotism in Panama?

REAGAN: No, no.

BUCKLEY: Yes. Well, you really *tried* to say that.

REAGAN: No. [*Laughter and applause.*] No, Bill, I really didn't, but I also have to point out something else about this. The canal and Panama are Siamese twins. Neither one could have been born without the other, and 90 percent of all of the industry and the population of Panama is on one side of that canal. We have the right to sovereignty, as we say, by that treaty. Panama had the worst riots of all in 1964. More than a score of people were killed. Yet not one move was made to attempt to sabotage the canal. Business didn't stop for one second, and a statement was made about those riots that said, "Led by persons trained in Communist countries for political action." The government of Panama, instead of attempting to restore order, was, through a controlled press, TV, and radio, inciting the people to attack and to violence.

BUCKLEY: Who was it who taught the people who did the Boston Tea Party how to exercise violence?

The evening moved briskly along, with our debating partners bringing in a useful variety of perspectives, until Senator Ervin sounded the warning bell as only he could:

ERVIN: The chair is going to have to interrupt. Personally, I wish this debate could go on till the last lingering echo of Gabriel's horn trembled into ultimate silence, but we are prisoners of time, and at this time, the chair is going to call on Governor Ronald Reagan for his rebuttal and is going to give the very sad advice that it has to end at strictly 10:44.

REAGAN: I have how long?

ERVIN: It's about ten minutes.

REAGAN: Oh, for heaven's sake. I don't know if I've got that much to say, Mr. Chairman.

Well, Mr. Chairman, and ladies and gentlemen: I think, again, we come back to the original premise that I was making here, and I would start, I think, with the question that I was unable to answer just now—the defensibility of the canal. If we're talking nuclear defense of the Panama Canal—if a missile is to come in aimed at the Panama Canal—then no. But you have to ask yourself, in the event of a nuclear war, who's going to waste a missile on the canal? They'll be dropping missiles on New York, Chicago, San Francisco, Los Angeles, and so forth, and it would be a waste of time to use that. So we come down to conventional warfare and we come down to sabotage.

I claim that the United States, with a military force trained on the ground, which has defended the canal against any attempt at sabotage through four wars, recognizing the fact that it's going to take more than a single saboteur slipping in in the night with a hand grenade or an explosive charge—it's going to take a trained demolition team, with plenty of time to work and no interruption, to do something to disable the gates, the locks, and so forth. Or the other means of sabotage would be to assault the dams that hold back the lakes—a two-hundred-square-mile lake, for one; there are three lakes—that provide the water that, through gravity flow, floods these locks. Now, I submit that with an American armed force on hand guarding those vulnerable points, they are far safer than if the Panamanians are in charge and the Americans are not there. . . .

Now, we have to face the Panamanians in a negotiation, *not* because we've been threatened that they're going to cause trouble—I say that this is one of the first things that should have called off the negotiations. When they threatened violence, I believe the United States should have said to them, "We don't negotiate with anyone under threats. If you want to sit down and talk in a spirit of goodwill, we'll do it." [*Applause.*] But we go back now and say, "If we can find a way that ensures our right to the security the canal must have, we'll do everything we can to find a way to erase the friction points." . . .

I don't believe that in Latin America we would do anything to strengthen our position by, again, yielding to the unpleasantness in this treaty. I think, if anything, we would become a laughingstock by surrendering to unreasonable demands, and by doing so, I think we cloak weakness in the suit of virtue. This has to be treated in the whole area of the international situation. The Panama Canal is just one facet of our foreign policy, and with this treaty, what do we do to ourselves in the eyes of the world, and to our allies? Will they, as Mr. Buckley says, see that as the magnanimous gesture of a great and powerful nation? I don't think so, not in view of an administration that is hinting that we're going to throw aside an ally named Taiwan. I think that the world would see it as, once again, Uncle Sam putting his tail between his legs and creeping away rather than face trouble. [*Applause.*]

Then it was my turn to sum up:

BUCKLEY: Mr. Chairman, Governor Reagan. James Thurber once said, "You know, women are ruling the world, and the reason they're ruling the world is because they have so insecure a knowledge of history." He said, "I found myself sitting next to a lady on an airplane the other day who all of a sudden turned to me, and she said, 'Why did we have to pay for Louisiana when we got all the other states free?'"

"So," he said, "I explained it to her." He told her, "Louisiana was owned by two sisters called Louisa and Anna Wilmot, and they offered to give it to the United States, provided it was named after them. That was the Wilmot Proviso. But Winfield Scott refused to do that. That was the Dred Scott decision."

She said, "Well, that's all very well, but I still don't understand why we had to pay for Louisiana." [*Laughter.*]

Now, intending no slur on my friend Ronald Reagan, the politician in America I admire most, his rendition of recent history and his generalities remind me a little bit of that explanation of how the state of Louisiana was incorporated into this country.

He says we don't negotiate under threats, and everybody here bursts out in applause. The trouble with *that* is that it's not true. We *do* negotiate under threats. Ninety-nine percent of all the negotiations that have gone on from the beginning of this world have gone on as a result of threats, as the result of somebody saying, "If you don't give me a raise, I threaten to leave my job." That's a threat, isn't it? What do you call what we did to George III? It was a most convincing threat. The fact of the matter is that there are people in Panama who don't accept the notion of Governor Reagan about the undisputed, unambiguous sovereignty that the United States exercises over that territory. . . .

We do have there the absolute right, which I do not deny and which my colleagues do not deny, to stay there as long as we want. But to say that we have sovereignty, as Governor Reagan has said, is to belie the intention of the people who supervised our diplomacy in the early part of the century, and it is also to urge people to believe that we harbor an appetite for colonialism which we shrink from, having ourselves declared in the Declaration of Independence principles that were not only applicable to people fortunate enough to be born in Massachusetts or in Connecticut or in New York or in Virginia, but people born everywhere.

And all of a sudden we find that we resent it when people say that they're willing to fight for *their* freedom. There was fighting done within a hundred yards of where we're standing here [in Columbia, South Carolina] because the people of the South felt that they wanted their freedom from the Union. We fought back, and it continues to be an open question whether there was successful diplomacy in the course of resisting that insurrection. But who is to say that the people who backed up their demands for freedom by saying they were willing to die for them are people for whom we should feel contempt? I don't feel that contempt, Mr. Chairman, and I don't think the American people feel that contempt either.

I think that Governor Reagan put his finger on it when he said the reason this treaty is unpopular is because we're tired of being pushed around. We were pushed out of Vietnam because we didn't have the guts to go in there and do it right, just as Admiral McCain said. [*Applause.*] We're prepared, as it was said, to desert Taiwan because three and a half Harvard professors think that we ought to normalize our relations with Red China. [*Applause.*] We are prepared to allow sixteen semisavage countries to cartelize the oil that is indispensable to the entire industrial might of the West because we don't have a diplomacy that's firm enough to do something about it. And, therefore, how do we get our kicks? How do we get our kicks? By saying no to the people of Panama. [*Laughter and applause.*]

I say: When I am in a mood to say no, representing the United States, I want to be looking the Soviet Union in the face and say no to the Soviet Union, next time it wants to send its tanks running over students who want a little freedom in Czechoslovakia. I want to say no to China when it subsidizes genocide in Cambodia on a scale that has not been known in this century, rather than simply forget that it exists. I don't want to feel that the United States has to affirm its independence by throwing away its powers—by saying we must not distinguish between the intrinsic merits of rewriting the treaty in Panama and pulling out of Taiwan because it is all a part of the same syndrome.

Who in this room doubts that if the president of the United States weren't Jimmy Carter but, let us say, Douglas MacArthur, and if the chairman of the Joint Chiefs of Staff were Curtis LeMay, and if the secretary of state were Theodore Roosevelt, and this instrument was recommended to the Senate—who doubts that the conservative community of America would endorse it? We are allowing ourselves to be beguiled not by those ideals to which we profess allegiance every time we meditate on the Declaration of Independence. We are allowing ourselves to express a quite understandable bitterness at the way we have been kicked around. We ought to be mad not at the Panamanian students who are asking for nothing more than what our great-great-grandparents asked for. We ought to be mad at our own leaders—for screwing up the peace during the last twenty-five years.

But do we want to go down and take it out on people who simply want to recover the Canal Zone? What we have done to Panama is the equivalent of taking the falls away from Niagara. Is it the kind of satisfaction we really feel we are entitled to, to proceed on that basis in order to assert a sovereignty which is, in any case, not a part of the historical tradition on the basis of which the Panama Canal was opened?

No. Let's listen to reason. Let's recognize, as Admiral Zumwalt has so effectively said, that we are so impoverished militarily as a result of so many lamentable decisions that we need the Panama Canal, and that we need the Panama Canal with a people who are residents of Panama, who understand themselves as joined with us in a common enterprise, because when they look at the leaders of the United States they can recognize that, not as a result of our attempt to curry favor with anybody, but as a result of our concern for our own self-esteem, we were big enough to grant little people what we ourselves fought for two hundred years ago. [*Applause.*]

A few months after the debate I was headed for the Reagans' house in Pacific Palisades for dinner. "Drive carefully as you approach the house," Reagan had warned me over the telephone. "I have special instructions for you on my driveway." I did as I was told. At intervals of twenty yards there were cardboard strips hand-painted with huge block letters. They read, in sequence,

WE BUILT IT.
WE PAID FOR IT.
IT'S OURS!

Well, the Senate *did* ratify the treaty, and the Panama Canal proceeded to operate just as smoothly as it always had. In other words, Ronald Reagan was, as a prophet, simply mistaken. And I, for my part, did not go on to be president.

# Correspondence, 1978

January 20, 1978

Dear Ron:

A hasty note. You were in marvelous form the other night, and whatever pleasure I took from the event, which had its transcendent disadvantage in having publicly to disagree with you, derived from what I hope was the obvious respect and admiration I feel for you. I profoundly disagree with the conclusions at which you have arrived, but I know that you credit my disagreement with you as sincere and thoughtful, and only wish I could say as much for some of your continuing fans, and some of my erstwhile fans! Remind me, at a moment consecrated to ribaldry, to relate to you and Nancy my conversation with Mrs. Frank Seaver on the subject.

With warm regards,
Bill

February 17, 1978

Dear Bill:

I'm just in from the "mashed potato circuit" with enough time to write at least a line or two in answer to your good letter of January 20th.

I know you "profoundly disagree" with my conclusions, and that is fair enough because I feel that way about your position. In fact, so much so, I'm going to get a lick in right now. Have you seen the testimony of our General Gordon Sumner Jr., chairman of the Western Hemisphere Inter-American Defense Board? He told a Senate committee our 18 Latin American allies are almost unanimously opposed to the treaties. It seems they all have internal Communist problems in their countries and believe Panama having the Canal will only make their problems worse. He then asked for early retirement. I burden you with this because I think it is extremely important, when we know our main adversary is the Soviet Union.

Enough of that--debate is over. The all important thing is what you mentioned in the opening lines of your letter--our continuing friendship. That is truly priority "numero uno." How about that--I'm a linguist (for two words).

Nancy sends her love, and give our love to Pat.

Sincerely,
Ron

## 12

# Reagan Anticipates His Presidency

By January 1980 Ronald Reagan was running hard for the presidency, but he was able to take a day off to appear another time on *Firing Line*.

In planning the program I thought it would be theatrically effective to ask him questions on the assumption not that he was a *candidate* for president, but that he *was* president—as indeed, one year and one week later, he was. (I had not warned him in advance that this was what I proposed to do.)

BUCKLEY: Those who oppose Ronald Reagan cite, exhibiting traditional American ingenuity, almost everything they can think to say against him. Careful attention is given to avoid citing his record as governor of the largest state of the Union, to which office he was re-elected—in a heavily Democratic state. Careful tabulation reveals that, in order of their frequency, Mr. Reagan is criticized (a) for having been born too long ago, (b) for being inexperienced in foreign affairs, (c) for standing by a series of propositions no different from those he articulated in 1964, and (d) for being lazier than other candidates, who travel more frequently to New Hampshire and Iowa.

These criticisms are difficult to confute objectively. If Ronald Reagan were to enter the 1980 Olympics and win the hundred-yard dash, there are those who would say that that was the last effusion of a discharging battery. If tomorrow he were to write a sequel to Machiavelli's *The Prince*, there are those who would say that here finally is proof that Ronald Reagan's mind is rooted in the Renaissance. If tomorrow he announced that in the next six weeks he would visit every town and hamlet in New Hampshire, there are those who would find here concrete evidence that Governor Reagan has finally recognized that he is not the front-runner.

Accordingly, I propose to spend the hour discussing not so much the forthcoming campaign, but rather: How would a President Reagan, were he now safely inaugurated, handle himself? What are the priorities that guide him? What techniques of government appeal to him? What is his view of the responsibilities of the chief executive? I shall offer him hypothetical problems.

I should like to begin by asking "President" Reagan: What would you do if, say, one afternoon you were advised that a race riot had broken out in Detroit?

REAGAN: Well, I would be inclined to say that that was a problem for the local authorities in Detroit, unless those local authorities were unable to control the situation and had called on the federal government for martial help. And maybe one of the things that's been happening too much is the federal government has been interfering where they *haven't* been invited in.

BUCKLEY: Do I understand you to say that the actual role attempted by, say, President Johnson during the riots of his administration might have exacerbated the situation rather than helped to mollify it?

REAGAN: Well, when I was governor of California, it was in the roaring sixties, when the campuses were in ferment, and we were talking about long, hot summers, and there would be more cities burned and more rioting. Those were handled, in the first place, by local authorities, even in war-torn Berkeley. The state was not involved until the local authorities—as they did one day, calling from the university president's office—told me, as governor, that they could no longer assure the safety of the people of Berkeley, and they asked for the National Guard, and I immediately sent the National Guard in.

In fact, this proved not to be an issue during 1981–1988. There were no race riots during Reagan's presidency to test the Reagan position on how to handle them.

I went on.

BUCKLEY: President Reagan, Tito is dead. The pro-Soviet faction in Yugoslavia has urged the Soviet Union, citing the Brezhnev Doctrine, to send its armies to restore order, and you are advised that in fact Soviet columns are on their way south.

REAGAN: Well, I would hope, by that time, the United States would have given enough signals to the Soviet Union, beginning with, say, Afghanistan—such as an American presence now in the Middle East; an American presence in the Indian Ocean and the Persian Gulf area; the restoration of arms sales to Pakistan and an American presence even there (because we have a treaty with Pakistan)—that the Soviet Union would have received enough signals that a move of the kind you've just described would run the very serious risk of a direct confrontation with the United States. And I don't think the Soviet Union *wants* a direct confrontation with the United States. . . .

I know that President Carter has said he's just discovered that the Soviet Union can't be trusted. That's something that a great many people would have been happy to tell him anytime over the last several years. . . .

There were times in the ensuing eight years—particularly over the Intermediate-Range Nuclear Forces treaty—when President Reagan seemed to me and to many conservatives to come perilously close to trusting the Soviet Union. But more of that in due course.

BUCKLEY: Representative Kemp of New York State proposes that all future United States bonds be issued on a guaranteed-purchasing-power basis. What is your reaction, Mr. President?

REAGAN: That sure would make the government honest for a change. Today we even use patriotism to induce people to buy bonds, and yet the federal government knows that as long as we maintain this inflation rate, they are going to pay the people back with dollars that, even plus the interest, will not buy as much as the dollars that the people who are investing in those bonds put up—

BUCKLEY: And then tax the interest.

REAGAN: —and then *tax* the interest. And of course the answer is to . . . stop inflation; and government should be doing that, and it hasn't. But yes, that sure would give the government something to think about. In other words, if it had to index and give back to the people dollars that had the same purchasing power as the dollars that they had invested.

BUCKLEY: Well, that is a very specific proposal that has been made by Milton Friedman. The notion is not to sell this as an anti-inflationary weapon, because it won't necessarily control inflation—

REAGAN: No.

BUCKLEY: —but at least it will keep the government from defrauding the people.

REAGAN: That's right.

BUCKLEY: It would also hugely lower the interest rate, obviously, because if you were going to get your inflation back, you'd be disposed to buy bonds at a lesser carrying cost.

REAGAN: Yes.

BUCKLEY: The carrying cost would be implicit in the sense that the government would have to bear the burden of its own inflation. Are you favorably disposed to such a reordering?

REAGAN: Well yes, because I've often thought, Bill, that— Well, last year the American people reported capital gains for tax purposes of four and a half billion. An economic study has revealed that those capital gains, if they were computed in constant dollars, actually represented not four and a half billion profit, but a one billion loss. Now, by what right does the government make you pay a tax on a *loss*? If we're to have a capital-gains tax, I think that tax should be computed in constant dollars. You shouldn't have to pay a tax on inflation.

BUCKLEY: So in brief, you would not veto any act by Congress that authorized the issuance of guaranteed-purchasing-power bonds?

REAGAN: No. I'd laugh all the time I was signing it. [*Laughter.*]

In fact, that was a reform that was never enacted, during the Reagan administration or since. On the other hand, the Reagan administration implemented indexation for the federal income tax, ending bracket creep—a reform judged by Milton Friedman (and others) as the most important of the Reagan administration.

BUCKLEY: Mr. President, the Department of Commerce announced yesterday that during the preceding quarter unemployment had gone to a level of 10 percent. What do you propose, by way of remedial action, to Congress?

REAGAN: Wait a minute. That unemployment had gone—

BUCKLEY: From 6 percent to 10 percent in the last quarter.

REAGAN: Well, that's probably due to some of the massive layoffs in the automobile industry, and again aren't we getting to a—

This was Reagan's only slip from the format I had devised, but he recovered quickly.

BUCKLEY: This is hypothetical, you understand.

REAGAN: What?

BUCKLEY: This is hypothetical.

REAGAN: Oh, this is *hypothetical.* Well, I don't think that *would* happen—

BUCKLEY: You can't challenge a hypothesis.

REAGAN: —in this administration that we're talking about—because by that time we would have gone to work—

BUCKLEY: But suppose it happened the day after you were inaugurated, so you could still blame the preceding administration?

REAGAN: And I would. [*Laughter.*] Without question, I would.

BUCKLEY: What would you propose, to turn the economy back toward fuller employment?

REAGAN: Well, we would start an immediate program of cutting income-tax rates across the board for everyone, to provide incentive for individuals. We would go after some of the punitive taxes and the tens of thousands of regulations which are keeping American industry from being as competitive as it could be in the world market. Our rate of increase in per-man-hour productivity is only a third what it is in Japan, half what it is in West Germany—not because our working people aren't as good as their working people, but because we have the highest percentage of outmoded industrial plant equipment of any of the industrialized nations. This is so because federal-government practices have kept us from having the capital we need to modernize, but what capital investment we do make is in answer to government mandates to meet environmental or safety standards, ideas that the bureaucracy has.

I have in speeches around the country been pointing out there are seventeen United States Steel Company plants closing in this country. We once produced 47 percent of the steel in the world.

We now produce 19 percent. But there are twenty-seven government agencies imposing 5,600 regulations on the steel industry.

I would also like to eliminate the tax on interest on savings accounts to encourage thrift, because the American people are saving at the lowest percentage of their earnings that they ever have saved and lower than the workers in other countries. Thus we're reducing the capital we have for research and development, to develop new products that will employ those people that are no longer needed in the steel mills and so forth.

If we'd do all of those things, I think we'd begin to see, because three times in this century—four times in this century, three times under Republicans, once under a Democratic administration—we followed that policy of an across-the-board tax reduction, and the burst of prosperity was so great that even in the first year the government got more money at the lower rates than it had been getting at the higher rates. And I just have faith in the *marketplace*, and I believe that this is the way we must go to curb inflation. This is the way we must go to put us back where we were as an industrial giant.

BUCKLEY: While you are encouraging these tax reductions, there is inevitably a deficit in the cost of government operations. This you would cope with how?

REAGAN: Well, since the General Accounting Office says that there's probably fifty billion dollars lost at the federal level alone through fraud and waste, we might start with that. That would certainly eliminate the deficit right now, if you could eliminate that. And from my experience in California as governor, I found out that you *can* eliminate things like that. Balancing the budget is a little bit like protecting your virtue: You just have to learn to say no. [*Laughter.*]

BUCKLEY: You would propose to say no to future programs, or would you say no retroactively, by asking Congress to repeal some existing programs? If so, which?

REAGAN: Well now, pardon me, but you've just reminded me of another facet of my program that I hadn't given as yet and I should have. Part of that program calls for a reimplementation of the Tenth Article of the Bill of Rights—the one that says the federal government shall do only those things that the Constitution calls for, and all others shall remain with the states or the people. I propose and would have already started, if your hypothesis is correct, a planned and orderly transfer back to the states and local communities of functions the federal government has usurped, and which it has proven it is incapable of operating. And one of the first of those would be welfare.

One of the second would be in the field of education. I would like to dissolve the ten-billion-dollar national Department of Education created by President Carter and turn schools back to the local school districts, where we built the greatest public school system the world has ever seen. I think I can make a case that the decline in the quality of public education began when federal aid became federal interference.

Well, the Reagan administration did indeed reduce income-tax rates, and these rate reductions did indeed increase federal revenues. But it turned out that these increases were vastly insufficient to balance the budget, at least in part because President Reagan's dreams of reinstituting federalism failed almost without notice. Specifically, no serious effort was made to eliminate the Department of Education, and no president since Reagan has even suggested such a thing.

BUCKLEY: Mr. President, yesterday the union of postal employees went on a nationwide strike. Now I know you well enough to know that your instinctive answer would be "How can you tell?" [*Laughter.*] Having got past that, what would be your official policy toward a strike by federal and municipal employees?

REAGAN: I have thought for a long time that by law they should not be allowed to strike. Government is not the same as private business. Government cannot close down the assembly line, and isn't it significant that when government employees first began to unionize, they had the support of organized labor, but then organized labor supported them only on the condition that their unions would contain a no-strike clause—their constitution, I mean—a no-strike clause. The public employees should *not* be allowed to strike. Government *can't* close down.

Here President Reagan's action matched exactly the words of Candidate Reagan. Six months into his administration he fired the air-traffic controllers who were striking illegally and endangering the public. His act deeply affected, in the desired direction, organized labor's routine disdain for the public.

We went on, through OPEC, the question of selling grain to the Soviet Union, and public expressions of religious belief—

REAGAN: Do you mean, bad as Congress has been all this time *with* praying, they want us to take it now *without* praying? [*Laughter.*]

BUCKLEY: I think that what you just said is so homiletic it might *itself* be unconstitutional. . . .

—and wound up with the CIA:

BUCKLEY: Finally, Mr. President, the CIA has complained to you that it cannot discharge some of the recent directives that the National Security Council has given it as a result of its having been hamstrung by a number of provisions initiated by Senator Church three or four years ago. How would you handle that dilemma?

REAGAN: Why, I'm surprised that they're complaining, because one of the first things I did when I took office was ask Congress to repeal those restrictions that were put on by Senator Church.

BUCKLEY: And what threats did you use if Congress didn't comply?

REAGAN: That I would take my case to the people and tell the people that we were flying blind with no counterintelligence whatsoever and that the Congress was to blame.

BUCKLEY: Thank you, Mr. President. [*Laughter.*]

# 13

# *National Review*'s 25th

April 28, 1980

Dear Ron:

   You will be relieved to learn that I do not wish to
be Secretary of State. You may be alarmed to learn
that I do not wish to be appointed ambassador
anywhere, which would have the virtue of getting me
out of the country when you decide to give away the
Erie Canal. You will be interested to learn that I do
not desire any jobs for any members of my family, and
that although I will make myself available for
consultation in the matter of future chief justices
of the Supreme Court, I will never initiate a
telephone call to you in such matters. I forgot to
tell you the price for all this, which is that you
must consent to be the guest of honor at our 25th

Anniversary dinner at the Plaza Hotel on December 5th.

It is probably the final formal celebration for which we will, so to speak, sit. After a while, it is seemly to privatize one's birthdays. But the 25th is very important, I think, and the symbolism of this one almost overpoweringly so. When we began publishing, the reception of the magazine is best described as derisory ("Scrambled Eggheads on the Right"--*Commentary*, by Dwight Macdonald). Today, every contender for the Republican presidential nomination acknowledges the principal emphases of *National Review* as we labored over the years to keep bright the tablets. Now we need--you; want you; won't take No for an answer. Think of it: twenty-five years it took us to put you in the White House! Ah, but it was worth it. So: *mark the date!* If I don't hear from you within ten days, write to me in Casablanca.

> As ever,
> Bill

Reagan enthusiastically accepted, and I thought no more about it, certainly not on the Glorious Fourth, as we took to calling it—November 4, when he carried forty-four states to President Carter's six, and the Republicans took control of the Senate for the first time in more than twenty years. It wasn't until a couple of weeks after election day that I thought to check with him on details for the evening and was told the devastating news: When someone is elected president, his civilian calendar, so to speak, is swept away. No record had remained of our celebration, and Reagan had been irreversibly scheduled for another event that evening. I was horribly disappointed, as were my colleagues, but there was nothing to be done. I made the best of the situation in my remarks at the Plaza Hotel, December 5, 1980:

This is a joyous occasion, and there are too many people to whom I and my colleagues feel gratitude to make it safe to name names, though in due course I shall make a single exception to The Rule. I elect tonight to abjure solemnity. It is barred from the proceedings. I reiterate Stan Evans's sentiments with respect to our missing guest, the president-elect. A few weeks ago I advised him that I had received the periodic form from *Who's Who* asking whether there were any changes I wished to make in my forthcoming entry. I asked the president-elect whether he would acquiesce in my contemplated change from "Profession: editor and writer" to "Profession: ventriloquist." He laughed. But he laughed longer than I would have done, and this persuaded me that, as a ventriloquist, I was a failure.

But I am not a total failure tonight: because I have been made to feel like an extension of the Equal Employment Opportunity Commission. When it transpired that the president-elect could not be with us, I received a telegram: "DEAR BILL: SORRY ABOUT THE PRESIDENT-ELECT. COULD I SUBSTITUTE? I'M ABOUT THE SAME AGE, WAS ONCE IN A TRADE UNION, HAVE PAST A.D.A. CONNECTIONS, AND, UNLIKE GOVERNOR REAGAN, I WILL ASSOCIATE WITH PRACTICALLY ANYBODY. ALL THE BEST. JOHN KENNETH GALBRAITH."

We would welcome Professor Galbraith to our ranks. *National Review,* like the White House, makes way for late vocations.

I note that I said to Miss [Deirdre] Carmody of the *New York Times*, rather weightily, that the role of *National Review* in the months ahead would be to attempt to measure the distance between the paradigm and the actualization of policy. (Grandfather, what big words you use!) It is part of the conservative philosophy to be grateful that no single person will ever achieve sufficient power to transcribe into public policy all the prescriptions of his own voice. Our journal, although it is primarily a vehicle for thought and analysis understood as conservative, is many other things, none of them conflicting. We seek to illuminate and to entertain, to criticize and to heighten the sensibilities. Inevitably, the observance of criteria as otherworldly as the injunction against coveting one's neighbor's goods means that success must be both partial and tentative. Mr. Reagan departs now from his sometime role as tablet keeper, to take up the role of executor of policies that, as is so often remarked, share certain elements with the sausage, namely, that familiarity with the processes by which they are made would kill the appetite for either.

Still, there is pleasure in even a little progress, even among those of us taught, at our mother's knee, not to seek to immanentize the eschaton.

The spirit is keener in America today than it was five weeks ago, and on this point I doubt that there is widespread disagreement. This is not because there is an abatement in the power of those who seek to destroy liberty, or an evanescence of such forces as bring lending institutions to ask for 18 percent interest on their money. We are revived by the enfranchisement of a fresh set of governors, with fresh recognitions of ancient vices and temptations. Ronald Reagan writes me, "After all, I've been reading *National Review* for twenty-five years"; and five years ago, in this hall, he said, "I want to express to *National Review* my appreciation for a fund of great knowledge that I've acquired." I take girlish pleasure, on behalf of the editors and writers at *National Review*, in that statement. Even while feeling the same embarrassment experienced by President Lincoln when, in a receiving line, a lady thrust into his hands a huge bouquet of flowers, leaving him physically paralyzed. His handling of the situation was exemplary.

"Are these really mine?" he asked.

The lady giggled with pleasure, and said, "Yes."

"In that case," said Mr. Lincoln, returning the flowers to his guest, "I wish to present them to you." With all gratitude to Governor Reagan, we make him a gift of that fund of great knowledge he has acquired by reading *National Review*.

# 14

# New Beginnings

My wife and I attended the first of the five or six inaugural balls to which the new president was indentured. And I have to confess that the dark part of me hoped that President Reagan would commit something like the largest gaffe I had heard in my lifetime, spoken twelve years earlier by the freshly inaugurated President Richard Nixon.

Time: January 1969. Place: One of those same ballrooms. Nixon had several such parties to attend in the course of the evening but clearly was in no hurry as he was handed the microphone by Guy Lombardo.

"It's just great to be here, especially under the circumstances." He grinned. "I remember VJ Day very clearly. Pat and I were outside the Roosevelt Hotel, and she saw a sign that said Guy Lombardo was playing, and she said she would like to hear him. The tariff was $15, and I said that was a lot of money to blow on one evening of music." He frowned. "But what the heck, we had just won a four-year war. Guy Lombardo." He turned to the band leader: "Let me tell you this: I hope to be able to hear you play at the end of the next world war."

But Ronald Reagan forswore any desire for another world war, even if it might have led to another evening with Guy Lombardo.

I had never been to the living quarters of the White House, where Mr. Reagan was confined for several weeks after the attempted assassination. There was the initial wholehearted embrace. Nancy stood, her arm in his as if his mere standing required her support.

And it was generally understood that this was so, as she never left his side, and we slid into the little dining room across the hall, about the size of a couple of Pullman dining tables. Reagan spoke with a steady lightheartedness, but this must have been hard. We did not yet know how severely he had been wounded, or how close he had come to catastrophe. He immediately led me back across the hall, to the little room in which he exercised every day, intending a physical rehabilitation which in fact he achieved within one year after he was shot.

Back to our spare lunch (no wine, I sadly noted), and the talk turned to the children. Ron was dancing with the Joffrey Ballet company, and Nancy detailed the miserable living conditions he was enduring, and the slender character of his paycheck.

It happens that I knew a fair amount about this because Ron and Doria had spent a weekend with Pat and me, intending to sail with us. I was astonished, after they drove in in their own car, to see the second car with four Secret Service men. But Pat had been warned, and we had our son's garage apartment available to make room for them. The comedy proceeded, as the four men mounted a rented Boston whaler to follow us across Long Island Sound to Oyster Bay, eight miles away. The wind was brisk, and Pat's sun hat blew into the water. Ron gesticulated wildly, pointing to the hat, and said to us: "They'll think it's mine and fetch it up," which is what happened. That night, as we ate our steak in the little harbor, he told us he intended to dismiss the Secret Service who kept their vigil near the tiny quarters he and Doria occupied on the West Side of Manhattan.

Doria said, "I'm not sure you can do that, Ron."

"We've had this argument before, Doria. It's up to us to decide who parks on the bottom floor of where we live."

Doria looked at me. I told her I did not have an answer to that constitutional punctilio, but that if they wished, I'd ask somebody at the Library of Congress. We all laughed, and indeed, a few weeks later, Ron dismissed the guards dispatched by the Secretary of the Treasury.

That was also on Nancy's mind at lunch, another example of filial loose-footedness and failure to harmonize with the requirements at the highest end of American life. Relations were not broken, but they were strained.

And then of course there was the endless matter of Patti. She was an unsilenced and evidently unsilenceable liberal, as the whole world could easily gather from the numerous profiles done of her. Her parents had heard that she was being pursued by *Playboy* magazine to appear as the nude starlet of a forth-coming issue (*Playboy* eventually succeeded, and her picture appeared in July 1994). This brought tears to the eyes of her mother. "I love my children, but I don't always like them," she said.

Reagan lowered his head a bit, and the jauntiness was gone. He said to her: "When they get into trouble, or have serious questions, they'll go to you."

In his first appearance on *Firing Line*, RR ponders WFB's question: Is it possible, in Great Society America, to be a good governor? C. Dickerman Williams, WFB's libel lawyer, serves as moderator.

California government may be as frenetic as a Marx Brothers movie but it's nowhere near as much fun.

*Firing Line* producer Warren Steibel (right) congratulates host and guest.

*NR* publisher Bill Rusher still wishes RR had gone for the presidency in 1968.

Conferring with Barry Goldwater before *NR*'s 20th Anniversary party. Three days later, RR will declare for president against Gerald Ford.

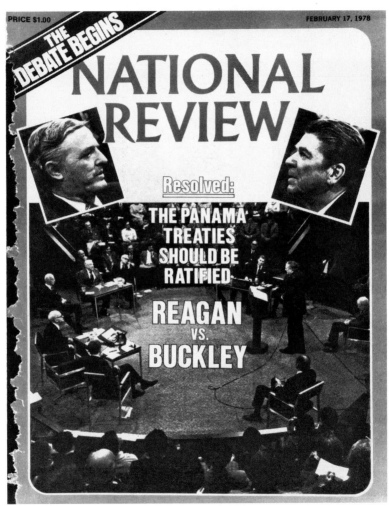

PRICE $1.00                                        FEBRUARY 17, 1978

THE DEBATE BEGINS

# NATIONAL REVIEW

Resolved:

THE PANAMA
TREATIES
SHOULD BE
RATIFIED

REAGAN
vs.
BUCKLEY

Jan Lukas

For *NR*, the Panama Canal debate was a very big deal.

When *NR* opened its Washington office in 1983, our favorite president came to welcome us; senior editors Richard Brookhiser, Priscilla Buckley, Joseph Sobran, and Jeffrey Hart look on.

At *NR*'s 30th, RR and Priscilla Buckley listen to WFB ask, Just how powerful is the most powerful man in the Free World? Jan Lukas

Dear Nancy, will we *ever* manage to meet in Casablanca?

An evening at the White House—Did you hear the one about . . . ?

Lunch at the White House—Mr. President, your ambassador regrets to inform you that things are not going so well in Kabul.

*NR*'s salute to the Reagan Revolution.

# *Correspondence, 1980–1981*

September 2, 1980

Dear Ron:

I was glad to hear from Henry that Mike Deaver
called him and that you will be meeting in due course
with HK,[1] the better to exploit his extraordinary
talents for the good of the republic. I understand
that the formula arrived at explaining HK's
unavailability for steady work for your
Administration is satisfactory to both parties.
Henry, on reflection, had a little difficulty with the
flat-out statement: I decline to be Secretary of
State. I tried to cheer him up by saying that I would
be glad to follow his statement with a public
declaration, "I withdraw my name from consideration
as King of England." Henry's sense of humor is equal
to any situation, as you know. Which reminds me that
a year ago I arrived in Hartford to give a speech to
somebody about something, and the press surprised me
by asking for a comment on Lowell Weicker's
announcement that morning that he was a candidate
for the presidency, and what did I think were his
chances? Providence was with me, because just the
night before, I had watched the British comedians

---

1. Henry Kissinger.

Dudley Moore and Peter Cook on the Cavett show,[2] and Cavett asked Dudley please to explain exactly what was meant by the doctrine of "the royal succession." Well, said Moore reflectively, "here's how it works. If tomorrow there was a nuclear war, and 55 million British were killed, Peter here"--he gestured deferentially to his collaborator--"would be queen." I and the press enjoyed ourselves hugely for a minute or so at Weicker's expense, and now it occurs to me that my ha-ha-ha may cost Brother Jim the Senate seat,[3] so concentrated is the loathing of Weicker for anyone whose name sounds like Buckley. On the other hand, Weicker's problem is that he really dislikes anything other than his own reflection.

Am off to London for a week, five hours of television with: Tony Benn (born Anthony Wedgwood Benn--I once wrote that his venture in autoproletarianization would only be complete after he drops the second "n" from his surname); Sir Keith Joseph, éminence grise to Beloved Margaret the Iron Lady[4]; a guy called Kelly[5] who is supposed to know more about OPEC than Dan Rather, though of course that is presumptive nonsense; and two hours with Malcolm Muggeridge, one of them, "Why I Am Not a Catholic." It would be fun if at the end of that one he went up in smoke, but that would leave me without a fifth show. Then I promote my last novel[6] for a

---

2. Dick Cavett's hour-long weekly talk show ran for six years on ABC, and then five years on PBS.

3. Jim Buckley was running for an open Senate seat in his home state, Connecticut. He won the Republican primary a week after this letter was written, but lost in November to Democrat Christopher Dodd.

4. Margaret Thatcher had become prime minister in May 1979.

couple of days. I note that the British edition omits mention, in the list of previous books, of *Saving the Queen*. There is no gratitude in this world.

Take care of yourself, my friend. And remember that HK has a jeweler's eye for geopolitical interrelationships. I attach the remarks[7] I made about him at a testimonial dinner at which the competition included Frank Sinatra and Bob Hope. These were reprinted in *National Review*, which of course makes it inconceivable that you haven't already read them. But have another look.

My love to Nancy, and tell her that your offer to me of the ambassadorship to Afghanistan with bodyguards of ten U.S. divisions is an easily penetrable scheme for keeping me away from my long-deferred tryst in Casablanca.

As always, with warm regard,<br>Bill

꒰     ꒰     ꒰

November 5, 1980<br>CONFIDENTIAL

Dear Ron:

This is the final occasion when I will address you by your first name. I take some satisfaction in

---

5. J. B. Kelly, author of *Arabia, the Gulf, and the West*.

6. *Who's on First*.

7. Reproduced in *Let Us Talk of Many Things*.

recalling that, sixteen years ago, I teased you by addressing you as "Governor," anticipating an event which came to pass. Obviously you didn't know when to stop.

I write this confidential letter on October 25, with instructions to my office to dispatch it if you are elected President of the United States. On the day this happens I shall be in Rio. (If it doesn't happen, I may stay there.) But I have a single thing on my mind, and it is that I must not plead with you with less than any claim I have on your friendship and common bond of loyalty to our cause, to take special caution to get help in selecting critical members of the new administration. I don't mean to be specific, and certainly don't mean to be critical of the splendidly qualified people who surround you. I say only this, that there are brilliantly qualified men and women--a few, not many--who should be consulted, indeed who should play an active role in making recommendations. What you need, obviously, isn't men who are seeking government jobs, but men who might be persuaded to take them. You know the difference from your experience in California. I want to suggest most conspicuously that you enroll the help of Evan G. Galbraith, my classmate at Yale, senior partner of Dillon Read, chairman of Goldwater forces in Europe in 1964, who combines a variety of talents difficult to reproduce. You should I think avail yourself of the advice of Irving Kristol. And, already on your staff, you should listen to recommendations from Tony Dolan. To the extent I can be helpful, I am, as I have been for almost twenty years, at your service. You will note that, in deference to your

high station, I keep my note short, and authorize
you to continue to call

> Your faithful servant,
> Bill

ҡ,          ҡ,          ҡ,

> December 16, 1980

Dear Ron (34 days of this left):

You were kind to write, and I assure you that all
is forgiven. It was quite an affair, full of warmth
and good humor, and is written up in the forthcoming
25th Anniversary Issue, which I hope you will look
at, not only for the festoonery, but for the
content.

It was good to catch a glimpse of you and Nancy at
Brooke Astor's, though such melees are inevitably
invitations to celebrate coitus interruptus. I
didn't even have a chance to tell you the one about
Bill Casey. ("Bill Casey is the only CIA Director
for whom it will not be necessary to provide a
scrambler.") Your toast was just right; your wife
looked radiant, and I have resignedly given up my
little apartment in Casablanca.

Now Ron: In the months and years ahead, I shall
probably feel the impulse to communicate a piece of
information or analysis to you maybe once or twice a
year. Such communications will be motivated
exclusively by a desire to pass along information I
think you would want to have. Over the years you have
always answered my letters. I appreciate this
greatly, but appreciate also that the magnitude of

your correspondence in the days ahead will make this impractical. Would you, then, consent to an arrangement? Unless I know that a letter I write to you will be read by you, constipation would seize me. Now we don't want this, do we? So: If you would make an arrangement with a member of your staff as follows, I'd be entirely satisfied. QUOTE. Dear Mr. Buckley: The President gratefully acknowledges your recent letter about the Zeitgeist. END QUOTE. This will mean to me one simple thing, namely that *you* have read my letter, on which no comment is expected, let alone required. If at the White House end it would help for me to scribble some code or other on the face of the envelope (e.g., Attn: Miss Whatnot), then Miss Whatnot has merely to advise me of this. If this arrangement is satisfactory, mark it down on your calendar.

We are off to the Caribbean for Christmas at sea on the same vessel I sailed across the Atlantic on. I have done a book on the trip,[8] and must go over the manuscript.

Pat joins me in affectionate greetings to you both. You will be in my prayers, along with the republic we both cherish.

> As ever,
> Bill

ר   ר   ר

---

8. WFB's second Atlantic crossing, in 1980, was done not on his own sailboat but on a chartered 71-foot ketch, the *Sealestial*. The book would be called *Atlantic High*.

OFFICE OF THE PRESIDENT-ELECT

December 30, 1980

Dear Bill:

Just off to Palm Springs for new year's, so will begin by wishing you and Pat a Happy New Year.

I have read your recent letter abut the Zeitgeist- -there now, you know I read that one as well as two more that are on my desk. I think the answer to getting letters to me would be simply address it to me in care of Helene von Damm. She's going to be my gal Friday as she was for almost eight years in Sacramento.

Incidentally, I know you won't be reading this Happy New Year greeting for quite some while, because you are out at sea someplace with boat and book.

I've passed the letter you sent with regard to Russell Kirk on to our transition team but must confess, from what I've seen in the past, I don't know how anyone could hold that post at the Court of St. James's unless he was possessed of personal wealth.

Well, you are writing and sailing and I'm reading- -*National Review*, and the account of the party I missed. Have fun and I hope we see you soon.

Best regards,
Ron

THE WHITE HOUSE
WASHINGTON
July 15, 1981

Dear Bill:

I appreciated very much George Will's letter
regarding Bob Bork. I am going forward on this first
court appointment with a woman [Sandra Day O'Connor]
to get my campaign promise out of the way. I'm happy
to say I had to make no compromise with quality. She
is truly excellent, and I believe will make a fine
Justice. But, so far, the person highest on the list
for the next appointment, which I hope will be soon,
is Bob Bork. If you don't mind, I'm going to show Bill
Smith, Ed [Meese], and the others George's letter,
which brings up a human side not normally available
when you are judging a man's qualifications. Let me
say, in our search, we found no one superior to him.

Thanks again for all your help, and congratulations
on the wonderful job you're doing in Kabul. As soon as
you have that cleaned up, maybe Namibia?

Nancy sends her love and please give our love to
Pat.

Best regards,
Ron

        ﻙ﹍       ﻙ﹍       ﻙ﹍

July 31, 1981

Dear Mr. President:

Forgive me the delay in acknowledging yours
concerning Robert Bork. By all means make any use
you wish of the letter from George Will. I agree with

you that character is a vital consideration in selecting a Supreme Court judge, and it is reassuring to know that Bork, on top of his majestic qualifications as a scholar, has the other also.

By the way, at the Grove I spoke at some length with Potter Stewart on the question of the nature of the grilling Mrs. O'Connor will receive. It is strange but true that there are no clear boundaries to what question may be asked, or answer refused. Stewart is going to let me have the record of his examination (he was given a very hard time by the Southerners, having been appointed shortly after *Brown* vs. *Board of Education*), and I'll try to write a few columns that might prove helpful. He predicts, you will be glad to hear, a virtually unanimous vote in favor. (Who said you can't win them all?)

Did you know that since you sent brother James,[9] sometime sainted junior senator from New York, to Pakistan with authority to commit three billion dollars in military credits, his children refer to him as "the merchant of death"? As in: "Ma, is the merchant of death here for dinner tonight?" I hasten to add that all of them are devout believers.

Your ambassador to Kabul would like to call one thing to the attention of the president. Mind you, I don't do this censoriously. But you have been pretty good on the matter of your campaign promises. So: where are the fifteen divisions you promised me? Sometimes it gets lonely, underground life in Kabul.

_____

9. As Under Secretary of State for Security Assistance, Science, and Technology.

THE REAGAN I KNEW

But I am stirring up plenty of trouble for them, you betcha. Don't bother to acknowledge.

My congratulations and affectionate regards to you both, in which Pat joins.

                              As ever,
                              Bill

- 146 -

# 15

# Stockman and the Budget

R onald Reagan was initially pleased by the White House routine—not so very different from what he had got used to in Sacramento, with this difference, that his word, however soft-spoken, was hereabouts final. It was final even when it was not fully understood, either by his lieutenants or by Reagan himself, who didn't pretend to linger over technicalities.

Reagan, arrived in Washington, was determined to do something in the direction of balancing the budget. His predecessor, Mr. Carter, had piloted the country into the highlands of stagflation. This meant that, simultaneously, the country was suffering from price inflation—the cost of living rising—and from unemployment. It was a part of the capitalist catechism that the two phenomena would not coexist. If there was a plethora of goods, exceeding the money supply, then the regular, reliable engines of competition would ease the upward pressures, bringing prices down. A reduction in the supply of goods would signal to the market a need to increase the supply: exit unemployment. During Carter's last year in office, the "Misery Index" (inflation plus unemployment) was over 20 percent.

Reagan was pleased to find in Washington, ready to handle the whole business, a young congressman, David Stockman, whose familiarity with the economic scene was widely acknowledged. He had done graduate work at Harvard, where for a period he was in the divinity school.

David Stockman, though only 34, had an air of self-confidence when engaged in whatever he undertook. One of his extraordinary assignments had been in the service of Reagan as surrogate debater during the campaign, taking the place of John Anderson in practice sessions. He had done very well. Reagan conceded that on a couple of points, "Candidate Anderson" had outpointed Candidate Reagan, who said he was glad that Stockman was on the right side. Reagan duly named the young man Director of the Office of Management and Budget (OMB) and put him in charge of the administration's grand plan—adumbrated by Candidate Reagan one year earlier on *Firing Line*—to cut tax rates and the budget and the deficit simultaneously.

Reagan's confidence in Stockman came to a soggy end when *The Atlantic* appeared on the stands in November 1981. In an extended interview with an editor of the *Washington Post*, Stockman put forward his views of the Reagan program. Those views included the statement, "It's kind of hard to sell 'trickle down.' So the supply-side formula was the only way to get a tax policy that was really 'trickle down.'" And this, about the budget process, "None of us really understands what's going on with all these numbers." The whole business, Stockman permitted the happily skeptical interviewer to conclude, was a brew of Reagan Sunshine and bits and pieces of orthodox freshman economics.

In the months ahead, administration representatives had to labor hard to finesse the objections raised by Stockman. Viewed singly, the proposals embodied in the Reagan program sounded fine, the young director of OMB said, but taken together they were out of harmony with one another. They would not, separately, have the impact desired—said Stockman—and would not advance the corporate grand plan. The grander the vision, the easier it had been to reassure the orthodox. Even Ed Meese and Michael Deaver, from the Old Guard in Sacramento, had been carried away by Reaganomics, or appeared to have been.

Stockman emerged as a young and learned political warrior casting about to deliver the republic from the disordered president who had appointed him. It was made to seem, for the Democrats eager to reject the popular president, as if the architects of the Reagan plan had got mixed up and designed a strategy for an alien country, with alien purposes.

Stockman was himself a prominent, though not mortal, casualty. When that issue of *The Atlantic* was released, Stockman went to the president, apologized, offered his resignation, was "taken to the woodshed" and then forgiven, and went back to work. But although Stockman was kept on as head of OMB until 1985, the skepticism had hardened.

Stockman enjoyed the arts of explication. He was fully challenged by Reaganomics. He described himself a few years later, in his autobiography, as a "radical ideologue." His conservative instincts brought him to criticize mostly the sheer size of the government President Reagan had inherited. Reagan, on *Firing*

*Line*, had talked about cutting "fraud and waste" in the federal government to get the deficit under control. But Stockman was right in realizing that the problem was far more entrenched. As I wrote in my column about Stockman's autobiography: "It took Stockman a very long time before he discovered that the Reagan administration, for instance, simply stopped thinking about Social Security as a malleable budget feature. If he had known that, he says, he would not have engaged in the struggle to begin with, for the very simple reason that the struggle was not winnable. . . . Unless Social Security is made to correspond to contributions to Social Security, you are left with an imbalance that mocks at the idea of the Reagan Revolution."

# 16

# A Self-Interrogation on the Size of Government

*"I have been asked to talk about the debate going on in Washington over the startling new approach to economic policy. One week ago I spent an hour on television with my old friend John Kenneth Galbraith. The nature of the economic revolution going on these days is best measured by my informing you that Professor Galbraith spent most of the hour talking about the dangers of inflation. If Ronald Reagan accomplishes nothing more, he will go down in history as having catalyzed a fear of*

*inflation in John Kenneth Galbraith, Edward Kennedy, and Tip O'Neill."*

**—From a commencement address at the Cornell University Graduate School of Business and Public Administration, Ithaca, New York, June 13, 1981**

Q : Is it anywhere plausibly denied that Ronald Reagan ran for political office pleading excessive government?

A: No, although distinctions are of course required.

Q: For instance?

A: Reagan never charged that more money was being spent on national defense than required. Students would acknowledge that a heavy part of the Reagan "deficit" went to national defense expenditures. In his first term, defense expenditures rose about 30 percent.

Q: You speak of "distinctions." What else?

A: You're not going to ask me to cite, for example, flood, famine, and pestilence?

Q: No. But go ahead with a list of other factors that increase the deficit.

A: Well, since your approach is comprehensive, one could cite longevity. If the life expectancy advances, so would that part of government devoted to the care of the aged, notably Social Security.

Q: Well, yes. But these are trivial demurrals. The longevity of the population, while it increased during Reagan's eight years in office, did not increase so markedly as to effect a significant rise in government spending. How then do you account for the rise, under Reagan, of the budget deficit, from $79 billion to $153 billion?

A: It is a factor in democratic government that pressure is brought to bear to finance, by federal spending, projects that commend themselves to the voters. Or more exactly, to *some* of the voters.

Q: But surely such pressures are to be resisted?

A: Yes. And success in doing so is properly measured by the relative rise in such expenditures. If the Congress votes a $100-million rise in farm subsidies and the executive succeeds in trimming that to $50 million, there is a measure of relative success. The deficit grows, but by less than it would have grown if the president had yielded completely.

Q: What does a failure to contain the rise in federal expenditures reveal?

A: In formal political language it means that the political power of the legislature was greater than the political power of the executive. When the forces that ask for more spending prevail, their success depends in some measure on their power to move against the traditional American ethos. We aren't here confining ourselves to mechanical means by which budgets can be reduced. There are more significant limitations.

Q: Such as what?

A: The economic stability of a country. A country that needs to borrow in order to finance a budget deficit needs to find an entity to borrow from. Conventional shortfalls are handled by the sale of government bonds. But these, of course, need to be marketable. It would be difficult for Ecuador to go too far beyond its manifest economic resources when seeking brokerage of a national debt. The point arrives when Ecuador has noth-

ing left that investors want which hasn't already been mort-
gaged.

Another means of national deficit financing is the inflationary
route. A hundred-dollar debt diminishes in weight to the extent
the dollar reduces in value. This is most graphically demon-
strated in a gold-standard perspective. If a country owes $100,
traditionally this was expressed in gold weight. If a country
needed to buy gold, the charge levied would correspond to the
value of the local currency.

Q: Well, the U.S. dollar is not under any such pressure—

A: No, not any longer. Let's simply grant the obvious, that the
way to stimulate the sale of a national bond is to increase the interest you are willing to pay on that bond.

Q: If a country is having no problem in selling its bonds, why
should there be a problem with a budget deficit?

A: Well, the bonds have to pay interest. To pay that interest
requires taxation. And taxation is of course a disincentive to production. If taxation were at 100 percent, production would be at
zero percent. So there is that question for the budget-deficit nation: How to continue to operate without depreciating the national currency?

Q: Was Reagan making those points when he railed against
deficit spending?

A: Yes. He was warning, among other things, of the perils of
taking the inflationary road, on which, of course, the country
was well along. In 1980, the national debt was $908 billion. Up
from $257 billion in 1950. In essence, Reagan was arguing for
the survival of an ethos—

Q: What ethos?

A: The ethos of self-subsistence. Reagan always believed that people should earn their own living, and that a country should too, and that a country that does so is entitled to its national independence. In pressing for a balanced budget, he was attempting to stop the government from adding weight to the burden of living costs—he was rejecting extra burdens.

Q: Well, yes, but what you call so dismissively "extra burdens" can give life to civilization. The creation and maintenance of museums, for example, should not be rejected as merely costly burdens.

A: Recall that Adam Smith, who generated the popular criteria by which we judge the matter of what government may properly do, ruled that the government has distinctive responsibilities, primary among them to defend the nation against aggression. But a secondary obligation is to preserve the nation's monuments. These obviously include the museum you're so anxiously fussing about.

# *Correspondence, 1981–1985*

Dear Mr. President:

Well I'll be damned. I didn't know that I last
wrote you from only a few miles away from the famous
launching pad of your career. If I had, I'd have
dropped everything I was doing and put in for a
position as a sports announcer. To be sure, I'd have
needed a little brushing up. On the other hand, no
one has a better excuse than I for not knowing who
won the World Series. I was, as you alone know,
tracking the enemy in the mountains of Afghanistan
while this was going on.

The Stockman affair is not serious if weighed purely
on a moral scale. It was a venture in narcissism, so
what else is new. It will damage the cause only to
the extent that the Democrats can successfully
parlay the notion that even the evangelists for your
program secretly doubt its prospects. Hidden in
Stockman's long piece is in my judgment the key to
your problems. It is this, that the financial relief
extended to the entrepreneurial class simply isn't
significant enough. Stockman, in his press
conference, said defensively to those who spoke of
benefits to "the rich" that 70 percent of the relief
was going to "middle-class and lower-middle-class"

Americans. Correct, and that is the salient
disability of the program. It has not widely been
noted that taxes will continue to consume 50 percent
even after the third year of your program. Compare
by contrast Milton Friedman's recommended cap of 25
percent--and his flat prediction that if this were to
happen, there would be no loss of revenue, because
people don't use up a lot of economic energy to save
twenty-five cents on the dollar. If only you could
devote one strong speech to killing once and for all
the notion that people who succeed commercially are
hurting their country.

I went to Washington and gave the speech at the
State Department on the occasion of Van Galbraith's
swearing in as your ambassador to Paris.[1] A fine
occasion, and once again I thank you for designating
him. He'll do splendidly. Did I ever tell you how
much I like Bill Clark?

Nancy called Pat the other day, to check out the
person you have in mind to replace Lee Annenberg. I
don't know her, but Pat does and thinks well of her.
On Wednesday, we'll be taking in *Nicholas Nickleby*
with Ron and Doria. I think it extremely important
every now and then to make a public appearance in New
York, to distract attention from my principal
preoccupation in Kabul. You will be very interested
in the information I have collected for you in that
exciting theater.

Take care, and promise not to give away the Erie
Canal. Remember, we built it, we paid for it, and it
is OURS!

---

1. See appendix, p. 251, "Remarks at the Swearing-In of Evan G. Galbraith."

Always with warm regards, and don't bother to acknowledge.

As ever,
Bill

P.S. Barbara Walters asked for my help in getting together one or two questions to ask you in the forthcoming interview. Here's one you may want to think about: "When the Constitution made the president commander-in-chief, the Founders envisioned a man leading an army or a fleet, and the worst that could result was a lost battle, or war. But in a thermonuclear age, constitutional authority seems to give the president the right to take steps that could result in the elimination of American society. Is it wise that a single man should exercise that much power?"

ⅸ          ⅸ          ⅸ

Saturday,
January 9, 1982

Dear Mr. President:

You were swell to call me in acknowledgement of my last letter, and it was fine to talk to you. A day or two later I had the unusual and unexpected pleasure of seeing son Christopher for an evening (George Bush was speaking in Bridgeport, so Christo was near home), and he told me of your hospitality to him at dinner, and of your expert guidance to the Men's Room. Thanks, pal. You are not only a splendid president, but a splendid friend.

Last night I was at Harvard, doing a television debate in the style of our own encounter (you remember, when I just barely prevented you from giving away the Erie Canal?). My principal opponent was John Kenneth Galbraith. The resolution was: "Resolved, this house approves the economic initiatives of President Reagan." Packed house, the whole bit. I was deeply distressed by the recurrent emphasis on your alleged favoritism for the rich. I think I know all the arguments, and I tried them all. The audience listened, sometimes appreciatively, but its enthusiasm was for the notion that you are plundering the poor, for the benefit of the rich. Galbraith said: "Mr. Reagan is obviously pursuing the old adage that if you feed a horse enough oats, some will eventually reach the sparrows." After I dissected his arguments during the rebuttal, I concluded: "If you feed a horse enough oats, not only will some reach the sparrows, some will also reach Mr. Galbraith."

I fear most on any domestic development this: that supply-side economics—a genuine liberation of the economy—simply won't be given a chance under existing law. Yesterday a fellow called MacKenzie, writing for the *Wall Street Journal*, showed that three families in South Carolina (the typical state, nowadays) earning $10,000, $20,000, and $40,000 per year, are going to be worse off, the Reagan Tax Plan notwithstanding, than they were under Carter. Sure, they'll be better off than they'd have been if you hadn't acted. But the tax reduction simply isn't enough to prove the point we all believe in. If the top tax were reduced to 24%, then you'd have a real chance for a sharp reversal, and greatly enhanced reportable, and therefore taxable, income. A nightmare is that in three years the bad guys will say: "Well, had enough? Reagan tried it, and it didn't work." What is needed is a way to communicate to the people that by encouraging men and women economically you are helping the less well off, not hurting them. You are the most successful communicator in America. Kindly accept this as an ORDER!

My colleagues in Kabul were enormously heartened by your statement on Afghanistan. We keep very quiet there, as you directed that we should do, but it is fine to get occasional encouragement from the President. You will perhaps have noticed that in order to secure my anonymity, I make it a point to be frequently in the United States. But I am always in touch with Kabul when that happens.

Am off for a week of television, book promotion (tell Nancy to read *Marco Polo, If You Can*, my latest Blackford Oakes thriller), lecturing, and the traditional weekend of skiing with Milton Friedman in Alta.[2] We'll toast your health there. Pat joins me in affectionate regards to Nancy and you.

As ever,
Bill

2. See "Alta, My Alta," in *Miles Gone By: A Literary Autobiography.*

February 2, 1982

Dear Mr. Ambassador:

Thank you very much for your kind letter. However, I must say, I regret not having seen that TV debate at Harvard. I know you're right about the campaign to make everything we do seem as if it's aimed at the rich. I don't know how we can lick this, other than continuing to shout back, particularly since the press gives far more space to the charge than they do to my reply. There have been a number of those stories using inflation and the increase in the Social Security tax to indicate that bracket creep and those other things will have the people not actually getting a tax decrease down the road a few years.

Let me remind you, we have always talked about a second tax program which will be one to redress some of the imbalances in the present system. It, of course, has been delayed by the present recession. I think some of the people who are complaining also have forgotten that once our program is complete, we are indexing the tax brackets.

Enjoy your skiing. Nancy and I are looking forward to that other kind of weekend--sun and sand. Nancy sends her love, and give that from both of us to Pat.

Sincerely,
Ron

🖎　　　🖎　　　🖎

March 24, 1982

Dear Mr. President:

This one is rather specially confidential, so kindly note this and use your judgment in the matter.

Three days ago I was in Paris for one day, and learned that Mr. Nixon and Ambassador Van Galbraith were scheduled to meet for one hour, 10 a.m. to 11 a.m. I was Van's guest, and he phoned over to RN to say that I was there and planned to come in at the beginning of the meeting to say Hi. RN's sec replied by phone to say that RN would be delighted if I would join the two for the whole of the meeting. I stayed for one half (I'd have stayed on, except that the reason for my going to Paris was waiting for me at 10:30).

The purpose of this letter is to relay the highlights of what RN said, which is interesting. Maybe even crucial.

Let me begin by saying that in the past ten years all of us have read so much about RN that dumps on him, that we tend to forget (or I do) his political skills. These are very marked. This was the RN I had seen, off and on, since 1958. His grasp of the whole political cosmos was (always assuming his reckonings are right) masterful. At least, masterfully delivered.

Here are the salient points:

--RR is doing well, but there are deficiencies.

--RR should not spend as much time as he currently does up front, defending his policies. He should devote that time to occasional big-time television appearances. E.g., when the subject of the budget is finally disposed of, RR should appear on television and announce the way it's going to be. He should limit himself to four or five press conferences per year.

--RR desperately needs (forgive me, Nancy) a "nut-cutter." By which, said RN, he means somebody who goes out there and simply slaughters the bad guys, most vulnerable of whom in every way is Tip O'Neill. The n-cutter has to be the kind of person who can engage the attention of the press, and who speaks with some authority about RR's programs.

--Well, now, who should this person be? Bush? Too nice in manner. Baker?[3] Came in from the wrong end, and doesn't in any event command the press, or sway audiences. Dole? He's good, but is himself ambiguous about RR's programs. Richards? Richards is so awful, quite apart from anything else, he should be dismissed. So for God's sake, who?

--John Connally.[4] There isn't anybody in the U.S. who could do it better.

--Speaking from what position? Stockman's. Stockman is discredited, because everyone is convinced that he doesn't believe in RR's programs. The OMB is the single most important position in the Executive. Would Connally take it? Dunno, but it would need RR to persuade him. What about his miserable performance in the primaries? An anomaly-

---

3. Howard Baker was Senate majority leader at the time, and Bob Dole was chairman of the Senate Finance Committee. Richard Richards, GOP national chairman, resigned his post a few months later and was replaced by Reagan's friend Senator Paul Laxalt of Nevada.

4. The former Democratic governor of Texas had served as Treasury secretary in President Nixon's first term. He formally switched parties in 1973 and made a run for the Republican presidential nomination in 1980. As of 1982 he was a private citizen, involved in Texas real estate.

-he's a terrific vote-getter. He was probably sunk
by his Israel speech.[5] "He needs an Agnew," RN said.
"He did it for me, and he was first-rate--check his
ratings back then. I did it for Ike. Ike was smooth.
But when I went all-out against the Dems, and they
went to Ike, he'd sort of shrug his shoulders, but
when he saw me, he'd say: 'Attaboy, Dick. More of
the same.'" What if Connally wouldn't? Well, RR
would need to find somebody who would do it. The Dems
are terrifically vulnerable, but there isn't anybody
out there in headline-country who's skewering them
with their own vulnerabilities. It's got to be
done.

    --What about RR's actual program?

    --It's fine--provided. Provided what? Provided *he
doesn't let up*. If he licks inflation, he'll be a
national hero, but it'll take time. They're worried
about November? Here's what's going to happen in
November. Congress, down 20 to 30. Senate, up 3 to
5--would be better if we had better candidates: but
there's no chance of losing the Senate. The voters
don't tend to blame senators for bad economic news.
The governors are who's going to be hit.[6] Remember
what happened to them in 1970. But forget it--the
important thing is to go through with it. Look, 100%
of the people are hurt by inflation, and a depression
in the 1930s sense simply isn't going to happen. But
if RR and the Feds back off too soon, then you'll

---

5. In October 1979, Connally warned an audience at the National Press
Club of Israel's "creeping annexation" of the West Bank.

6. In the event, the Republicans lost twenty-six House seats (the worst
mid-term loss since 1950) and seven governorships; they held steady in the
Senate.

have monetary relief, and back to inflation. I know that RR won't back off. The thing is to keep the team together. If he does, let me tell you: 1984 will be a Republican dream. RR can stay in as long as he wants.

Question: Would your ambassador to Afghanistan relay the above if he didn't himself agree with it? Well, I think you know that I would, because RN is a terribly gifted political tactician, and when he isn't President, he's awfully good on most issues. Anyway, I think he is correct in all of the above, and thought you ought to have it.

Me: "Mr. President, hi! Believe it or not, the last time we had a personal conversation was on the China Wall."

RN: "You mean it was that long ago? Ten years?"

Me: "Yup. It was the night after we saw the ballet in Peking. The one Henry Kissinger in his book described as: 'The most stultifyingly boring three hours of my life. I don't remember the plot, but I think the girl married the tractor, and they lived happily ever after.'"

RN: "Yeah, I remember. She looked like a tractor herself. No wonder."

Will you forgive me if I postpone for a future communication my report on Kabul? Perhaps at Barbados. My love to Nancy, in which Pat joins.

Bill

᠁     ᠁     ᠁

December 13, 1983

Dear Mr. President:

That was swell of you to send me so warm a birthday greeting. Only you would have phrased it so kindly. Tony Dolan always tells me that the best stuff is what flows out of your own pen, and I believe him. I told Nancy I thought your stay-fit piece in *Parade* was marvelous. It tells a lot in brief catches, and is infectious in tone. Having said that, I rather wish I had not read it because it serves to remind me how inadequate my own regimen is. I try to bicycle twice a week, and once a week I do the gym work. But the idea of giving up salt is--well, it is un-American, Mr. President, and I hope that you will interrupt your tirades against salt for long enough to remember that our forefathers fought to make salt available to us untaxed. I wonder, if they threw Tip O'Neill into Boston Harbor, would he float?

Serious-business-wise, I thank you for your invitation to attend the Chinese banquet, which I had to turn down because I am speaking that night in Florida. I confess I worry about the Chinese business. One of these days, perhaps seven or eight years down the line, the Taiwanese need to declare their independence of the mainland, and pop up in the international order as a fresh and independent state. But until that happens, nothing should ever convey the notion that we intend to permit Taiwan's forcible annexation by the Chinese Communists. I know you intend nothing of the sort, but the Chinese Communists are exerting mighty pressures to suggest that in due course this is inevitable. I hope you will avoid any gesture, here or in Peking, that can be magnified or misinterpreted as suggesting that

U.S. determination to maintain Taiwanese independence is eroding. Why not ask Ed Meese to say that Peking's hunger for Taiwan is synthetic?

So, another year has gone by. I can't pretend I swing with all your decisions, but with most of them I do most heartily. And as long as I live I shan't forget all the personal kindnesses you and Nancy have paid me and Pat, who joins me in affectionate greetings and all the best for a happy and holy new year.

Bill

✎    ✎    ✎

February 2, 1984

Dear Mr. President:

I owe you a letter, and I have several things for you of interest, pursuant to your telephone call. But forgive me if I restrict this note to telling you how greatly excited we all are by the news that George Bush has nominated Whittaker Chambers for a Medal of Freedom. I write in the earnest hope that you will approve this nomination, feeling as I do that Whittaker Chambers was the most eloquent poet of freedom in the postwar period in America-- precisely because, as André Malraux said to him, "You did not return from hell with empty hands." No, he returned from the hell of Communism with a heart full of horror for what he had engaged in, and a determination to strive to help his countrymen avoid that horror. You may remember that when you spoke at *National Review*'s 20th Anniversary you quoted

Whittaker Chambers's haunting sentiments about the
death of the West, and how all that we could do was
to snatch a fingernail of a saint from the rack to
prove that, at the great nightfall, there were those
who cared. Well, giving Whittaker Chambers a
posthumous Medal of Freedom does as much as any
gesture I can think of to bring light, against such a
nightfall.

As ever,
Bill

✒     ✒     ✒

May 30, 1984

Dearest Nancy:

It was such splendid fun being with you for a
couple of hours. It is one of the few redecminy
features of public dinners that if one is seated
next to an old pal, he/she can talk about Casablanca
almost as privately as though they were seated in a
canoe on a lake in the middle of Central Park. It was
good catching up, and I have made a note to fetch up
the copy of *People* magazine with the spread on Ethel
and the children. Meanwhile, I look forward to
getting from Ron a copy of his interview with Our
Leader.

I am informed by a hysterically pleased Mona
Charen that you have taken her on your staff on a
trial basis for 30 days. Perhaps she told you that
she is a protégée of mine and of sister Priscilla.
She was the editor of the Columbia Year Book and the
only conservative in the University. She interviewed

me, and struck me as so intelligent and charming that when, a few months later, she applied for a job as an editorial assistant, I took her on, and she served marvelously for two years, before going on to law school. I remember that one of the questions she asked during the interview was: "If you were a woman, what would you do?" To which my reply was, "I would seduce John Kenneth Galbraith and bring him to his senses." She is devoutly Jewish, and did a stint in Israel before going to Law School. A marvelous sense of humor, a marvelous writer, and a bloody joy to be around. Hope you like her.

You probably won't see this until after you return from Europe. My prayers will be with you and El Maximo.

All love,
Bill

December 20, 1984

Dear Mr. President:

I thank you hugely for your letter, and apologize for the delay in replying. This will be brief, for reasons I spare you the knowledge of. I wished to record only that I accept your reappointment as ambassador to Afgh-n-st-n, on the understanding that it be kept, as before, completely secret. I was rather astonished over the telephone last week to discover that the First Lady knew about it. Is she to be trusted? Do not, please, tell her that I asked, because I am quite devoted to her.

And the second point: Kindly, Mr. President, circle December 5, 1985, on your calendar. Please do not let anyone else do this for you, because we remember what happened four years ago, when we celebrated the 25th Anniversary of *National Review*, and the president-elect was not in our company, and left us all feeling like Cinderella. On the assumption that between now and then you have not given up the Erie Canal--which we built, we paid for, and is ours--you will be our guest of honor.

Pat (whose improvement[7] proceeds only at moderate speed) joins me in affectionate greetings to you and Nancy. Bless you both, always,

Bill

꒰  ꒰  ꒰

January 22, 1985

Dear Nancy:

This is a love letter.

When El Presidente was sworn in, and after he spoke, I was standing five feet behind him--and you. And I saw your fingers caressing his. You thought the gesture entirely private, but I have Eyes That See All, and I was not, in living memory, so moved by so tender a liaison between a great leader and his incomparable wife. . . . But that wasn't all. That morning (Monday) I caught you on the *Today Show*. Now I like Bryant Gumbel. But he asked you all those tedious questions, and the wonderful moment came

---

7. From her second hip-replacement surgery.

when you said: Enough. Cut it out. Move over. I was truly pleased. The First Amendment to the Constitution, unless occasionally someone moves forward other considerations (privacy; dignity; reserve) becomes a bog, sucking in everything, in its insatiability: losing all perspective. Your impatience was galvanizing. . . . And, dear Nancy, thanks for being so kind to Pat. She has been terribly depressed by her illness, and your visit was a great tonic. It didn't help today to see the *Washington Post* with a picture of Clare Luce and me with the caption, "William F. Buckley Jr. and his wife Patricia arrive at the Capitol for the swearing-in ceremony in Statuary Hall."

Much love from,<br>Casablanca Bill

&#x1F598;   &#x1F598;   &#x1F598;

May 20, 1985

Dear Mr. President:

Well now, I greatly appreciate your calling me to say that you approved the treatment of the Bitburg business in *NR*.[8] On this one, I truly think we will win. My judgment reduces to a highly manageable distillation: the best way to prove we are enduringly resentful over the demonic treatment of human beings by the Nazis is to document--in a sense as a matter of honor to the fallen Jews--our determination to prevent the same kind of thing happening to others, without reference, as the saying goes, to race, color, or creed. I don't know how the English language can do that more eloquently than you did in your speech at Bitburg: utterly memorable. Both the text and the delivery.

Interesting point, the flak you ran into. Henry Kissinger, in a conversation with me, responded to my point that the opposition was a poignant statement of the continued insecurity of the Jews by adding that it was more than this, namely an arrogance, strategically at odds with the highest interest of any minority subject to persecution. The highest density of anti-Semitic persecution in the world today is in the Soviet Union. And the most eloquent voices favoring a tough anti-Soviet policy include a high percentage of Jews. To mention Norman Podhoretz and Irving Kristol and Leonard Garment merely suggests the point. The tragedy is the diffusion of effort done by the unbalanced opposition to Bitburg, given the circumstances that made Bitburg essential.

Great heavens! I do believe I am lecturing to you! I haven't done that since I endeavored to show you the error of your ways in respect of the Panama Canal Treaty. In most other respects you have been a pretty good soldier-philosopher, and I am proud to be your friend, and supporter. And, by the way, I do hope you will read the little essay I wrote to adorn

---

8. In the course of a European trip, Reagan had been scheduled to visit a West German cemetery in the company of Chancellor Helmut Kohl, to commemorate the fortieth anniversary of the defeat of the Nazis and celebrate forty years of U.S.–West German friendship. Word had got out ahead of time that the cemetery chosen, Bitburg, held the bodies of some four dozen SS men among two thousand German soldiers, and American Jewish groups had demanded that Reagan cancel the ceremony. Partly to avoid embarrassing Kohl, but more importantly for the reasons WFB adumbrates above, Reagan went ahead with the visit as planned.

the pages of *Vanity Fair*, showing you and Nancy
being really uppity.[9] I mean, being President of the
United States and First Lady is okay, but coming on
as Fred Astaire and Ginger Rogers--have you no sense
of modesty? Pat joins in affectionate regards to you
both.

> As ever,
> Bill

　　　　ら　　　　　　ら　　　　　　ら

November 6, 1985

Dear Mr. President:

Well now, I will be seeing you, unless the United
States Post Office performs a miracle, before you see
this letter. Please remember, when you introduce me
to Princess Di, not to reveal that I am your
clandestine ambassador to Afghanistan. I know that
from all indications she is not a security risk: but
we professionals like to take every precaution. As
for me, I shall endeavor in the course of the
evening's conversation not mistakenly to lapse into
Afghan. Becomes harder and harder to do, such being
my preoccupation with duty.

I hope you saw the piece I wrote after your UN
speech. But on no account are you to miss the one I
just finished writing, in which I refer back to the
continuing relevance of that terrific speech. So I am
enclosing a copy.

––––––––––––

9. This essay, "Nancy and Ronald Reagan," is reprinted in *Happy Days
Were Here Again.*

Nancy elects to get her little doggie[10] after the
*NR* Party on December 5. He is really quite lovable,
and entirely blasé about going to live in the White
House. The affair on the 5th will be quite splendid,
thanks largely to you. Oh, by the way, I'm glad
you're bringing along 100 assistants: I wouldn't
want you to be lonely! Chuck Heston will be the m/c
for half the program, Bill Rusher for the other
half. Tom Selleck is coming. All music, speeches,
etc., will be done, and my goal is for the affair to
end at 10:40. How do you like that for an impresario?
Perhaps you will retain me as such after you finally
pull me out of that wretched country you've had me
in.

It will be swell to see you. And thanks for
anything you can do for Steve Williams, who belongs
on that 10th Circuit: one of the finest young legal
conservative scholars in the country. I rejoice that
you've got Jim Buckley and John Noonan and Dan
Mahoney. By God, before you're through, you might
even reinstitute the Constitution of the United
States. Not bad for two terms.

Pat joins me in affectionate greetings to you and
Nancy.

As ever,
Bill

10. The Reagans' previous dog, a Bouvier des Flandres named Lucky, had
proven too rambunctious for the White House and was sent out to Rancho
del Cielo. The Reagans had admired the Buckleys' Cavalier King Charles
spaniels, so when Bill and Pat were acquiring a new puppy for themselves,
Loewy, they also took one of his littermates, Rex, for Ron to give to Nancy as
a Christmas present.

## 17

# National Review's 30th

This time, there was no slip-up. The ballroom of the Plaza Hotel was full, the flowers were abundant, the wine warmed and exulted us, the music was buoyant. Finally the doors at the end of the room opened and the guest of honor walked out, Nancy Reagan at his side. The President was shown to the head table, while I escorted Mrs. Reagan to my table. The crowd roared, then stilled for grace, and a hymn-like minute of music.

Two hours later, the President having spoken warmly and generously, my turn came to give, as host, concluding thoughts on the evening and on our guest, President Reagan.

Dwelling on it years later, I was prompted finally to explore what I said and its larger meaning. My purpose here is philosophical and historical. I had acted for many years, indeed most of the world had done so, on a premise which I celebrated that night as the primary agent for United States independence under the Soviet threat. We were safe (I said) because Reagan was Reagan, meaning, in this instance, a non-ambiguist on the critical question of deterrence. What I said in as many words, dressed up for the party, was that Reagan would, if he had to, pull the nuclear trigger.

Twenty years after saying that, in the most exalted circumstances, in the presence of the man I was talking about, I changed my mind. Whether that change will in any way influence policy in the years ahead can't be said. But you may agree on the importance, to this author, at any rate, of the revised thinking. Mr. Reagan is not here to tell us—and I doubt that he told anyone in his circle—that the critical moment having arrived, he would in fact *not* have deployed our great bombs, never mind what the Soviet Union had done.

"Why?" I heard Henry Kissinger say one night when the conundrum was discussed. "After all, what's the use?"

Here are the robust words I spoke, facing the President, that night in 1985. Not a tremor of protest was voiced by anyone, that evening, or after. I had, after all, merely affirmed the settled policy of the United States. But people still discuss Hiroshima, asking, more than sixty years later, whether the bomb should have been dropped. A fortiori, thinkers who define foreign policy and plan future modes of defense will have to wonder whether the deterrent we leaned upon (a) was legitimate and (b), after all, was credible. Would he, Ronald Wilson Reagan, have dispatched a flotilla of ICBMs to punish the aggressors?

The speech I gave is exactly reproduced here. The levity here and there gave it life that night and does, I think, even today.

Expressions of gratitude can be most awfully trying to the ear of an audience, generally captive. But the act of gratitude nowadays is probably more often neglected than overdone. We published recently in *National Review* an essay on patriotism, in which the author made the same point rather more ornately than Edmund Burke did when he observed that a country, in order to be loved, must be lovely. Professor Thomas Pangle concluded that there is plenty in our Constitution that justifies love of country; and, indeed, if the life we live here is not significantly different from the life they live over there, then George Kennan & Co. are correct that we oughtn't to keep nuclear weapons in our deterrent inventory.

Jonathan Schell shocked the moral-literary world two or three years ago when he counted up and advised us that the explosive energy of the combined nuclear resources of the superpowers amounts to eight hundred million times the power of the bomb that went off over Hiroshima forty years ago. I remember that when I read that figure it conjured to my mind not so much the awful destructive potential of man as the infinity by which we measure the value of what we have, over against what it is that, otherwise, we would not have. The President, speaking at a great graveyard in Germany last May, reminded us forcefully of the terminal consequences of engaging, whether willingly or by conscription, in massive, ugly efforts to take from others their lives, their fortunes, and their sacred honor.

A year before *National Review* was founded, I spent an evening with Whittaker Chambers, and he asked me, half provocatively, half seriously, what exactly it was that my prospective journal would seek to save. I trotted out a few platitudes of the sort one might expect from a twenty-eight-year-old fogy, about the virtues of a free society. He wrestled with me by obtruding the dark historicism for which he had become renowned. *Don't you see?* he said. *The West is doomed, so that any effort to save it is correspondingly doomed to failure.* I drop this ink stain on the bridal whiteness of this fleeted evening only to acknowledge soberly that we are still a long way from establishing for sure that Whittaker Chambers was wrong. But that night, challenged by his pessimism, I said to him that if it were so that providence had rung up our license on liberty, stamping it as expired, the Republic deserved a journal that would argue the historical and moral case that we *ought* to have survived: that, weighing the alternative, the culture of liberty *deserves* to survive. So that even if the worst were to happen, the journal in which I hoped he would collaborate might serve, so to speak, as the diaries of Anne Frank had served, as absolute, dispositive proof that *she* should have survived, in place of her tormentors—who ultimately perished. In due course that argument prevailed, and Chambers joined the staff.

To do what, exactly? The current issue of *National Review* discusses of course the summit conference, the war in Afghanistan, Sandinista involvement in Colombia; but speaks, also, of the attrition of order and discipline in so many of our public schools, of the constitutional improvisations of Mr. Rostenkowski,[1] of the shortcomings of the movies *Eleni* and *Macaroni*, of the imperatives of common courtesy, of the rele-

---

1. Democratic congressman Dan Rostenkowski, chairman of the House Ways and Means Committee, was attempting to mangle Reagan's tax-reform package.

vance of Malthus, of prayer and the unthinkable, of the under-rated legacy of Herman Kahn. The connections between some of these subjects and the principal concerns of *National Review* are greatly attenuated. Attenuated, yes, but not nonexistent: because freedom anticipates, and contingently welcomes and profits from, what happens following the calisthenics of the free mind, always supposing that that freedom does not lead the mind to question the very value of freedom, or the authority of civil and moral virtues so to designate themselves. There are enough practitioners in this room to know that a journal concerned at once to discharge a mission and to serve its readers needs to be comprehensively concerned with the flora and fauna of cultural and political life. We have done this in *National Review*, and because we have done this, you are here—our tactical allies, most of you; our strategic allies, all of you.

How is our cause being handled by our guest of honor? Two or three years ago I was asked by the Philadelphia Society to speak on the theme "Is President Reagan doing all that can be done?" It was a coincidence that my wife, Pat, and I had spent the weekend before with the President and Mrs. Reagan in Barbados, and I remembered with delight a conversation I had with my host on the presidential helicopter taking us to our villa the first evening, before the two days reserved for bacchanalian sunning and swimming on the beach in front of Claudette Colbert's house, where we would spend the day. I leaned over and told him I had heard the rumor that the Secret Service was going to deny him permission to swim on that beach because it was insufficiently secure, and asked whether that were so.

Helicopters, even presidential helicopters, are pretty noisy, but I did hear him say: "Well, Bill, Nancy here tells me I'm the most powerful man in the Free World. If she's right, then I will swim tomorrow with you."

Which indeed he did. I digress to recall that during one of those swims I said to him, "Mr. President, would you like to earn the *National Review* Medal of Freedom?" He confessed to being curious as to how he would qualify to do this, and I said, "Well, I will proceed to almost drown, and you will rescue me." We went through the motions, and I have conferred that medal on him, *in pectore*.

I told the Philadelphia Society that the most powerful man in the Free World is not powerful enough to do everything that needs to be done. But I speculated on what I continue to believe is the conclusive factor in the matter of American security against ultimate Soviet aggression, which is the character of the occupant of the White House, the character of Ronald Reagan. The reason this is so, I argued, is that the Soviet Union, for all that from time to time it miscalculates, has never miscalculated in respect of matters apocalyptic in dimension. And the Soviet Union knows that the ambiguists with whom it so dearly loves to deal are not in power at this time. So that if ever the Soviet Union were tempted to such suicidal foolishness as to launch a strike against us, suicidal is exactly what it would prove to be. The primary obstacle to the ultimate act of Soviet imperialism is the resolute determination—to repeat my own formulation—to value what we have, over against what they do not have, sufficiently to defend it with all our resources.

Ronald Reagan, in my own judgment, animates his foreign policy by his occasional diplomatic indiscretions: because, of course, it *was* a diplomatic indiscretion to label the Soviet Union an "evil empire." Ce n'est que la vérité qui blesse: It is only the truth that wounds. And he correctly switches gear, as required, when wearing diplomatic top hat and tails. He did not talk the language of John Wayne—or of Thomas Aquinas—while in Geneva. But how reassuring it is for us all, every now and then, to vibrate to the music of the very heart-strings of the leader of the Free World, who, to qualify as such, has, after all, to feel a substantial commitment to a free world. When the President ventures out to exercise conviviality with the leader of the Soviet Union, the scene is by its nature wonderful, piquant. It brings to mind the Russian who, on discovering that his pet parrot is missing, rushes out to the KGB office to report that the parrot's political opinions are entirely unrelated to his own.

Mr. President, fifteen years ago I was interviewed by *Playboy* magazine. Toward the end of the very long session I was asked the question, Had I, in middle age, discovered any novel sensual sensations? I replied that, as a matter of fact, a few months earlier I had traveled to Saigon and, on returning, had been summoned by President Nixon to the Oval Office to report my impressions. "My novel sensual sensation," I told *Playboy*, "is to have the president of the United States take notes while you are speaking to him."

You need take no notes tonight, Mr. President. What at *National Review* we labor to keep fresh, alive, deep, you are intuitively drawn to. As an individual you incarnate American ideals at many levels. As the final responsible authority, in any hour of great challenge, we depend on you. I was nineteen years old when the bomb went off over Hiroshima, and last week I turned sixty. During the interval I have lived a free man in a free and sovereign country, and this only because we have husbanded a nuclear deterrent, and made clear our disposition to use it if necessary. I pray that my son, when he is sixty, and your son, when he is sixty, and the sons and daughters of our guests tonight will live in a world from which the great ugliness that has scarred our century has passed. Enjoying their freedoms, they will be grateful that, at the threatened nightfall, the blood of their fathers ran strong.

# 18

# On Nuclear Strategy
# in Honolulu

*"In the West there were, everywhere, steadfast
friends of liberty, but by no means can it be
said that they dominated the public policy of
the West. That can be said of only one figure. It
was Ronald Reagan, history is certain to confirm, who suddenly forced the leaders of Soviet
Communism to look in the mirror, and what
they beheld was their advanced emaciation.
The Western superpower, thought to have been
castrated by the defeat in Vietnam, was busy
deploying theater nuclear weapons in Europe,
shattering any prospect of Soviet ultimatums
directed at Bonn, Paris, and London. More-*

*over, the leader of the bourgeois world was de-*
*termined to launch a program which the tech-*
*nological genius of America would almost*
*certainly have caused absolutely to frustrate a*
*Soviet first strike, and therefore any political*
*advantage from threatening such a strike. It*
*was, moreover, the same leader who had resur-*
*rected the moral argument, so successfully*
*neutered by a generation of ambiguists. He*
*spoke of the Soviet Union as an* evil empire! *He*
*said that history would consign Communism to*
*the ash heap: transforming Lenin's own words*
*as an ode to historical determinism!"*

—*From a lecture at Vanderbilt University,*
*Nashville, Tennessee, September 18, 1991*

C lare Boothe Luce enjoyed coming up with fundamentalist
formulations "which can truly clear the mind." She sat in
her elegant silk evening dress, in her waterfront mansion in
Honolulu. Here, in the large living room, open at the south
end to the sea and the elements, her guests, so often the high
and the mighty, were always welcome. The understanding was
that they would give over plenty of time simply to listening to
her.

This was not difficult to do, because although she often spoke
in very long gulps, she threw light on tangled questions by deriv-
ative hyperbole. Tonight she was hostess to only one guest, Cap

Weinberger, secretary of defense in the cabinet of President Reagan. Arriving in Honolulu on his own Boeing 707, he was en route to Jakarta for one of the periodic meetings with Asian leaders.

Clare Luce's cigarette holder was poised, a baton at a dress rehearsal. She arrested loose conversation about missile deployment by saying, "The trouble with our Chief Executive, Cap, is that essentially he doesn't believe that anyone should use force if there is a chance that somebody might get killed."

Weinberger didn't think that piquancy inherently objectionable, never mind that he exercised administrative responsibility over a vast American arsenal of nuclear weapons. Instead he smiled and tilted his head to one side, as he tended to do when framing a comment. But Clare stopped him, raising her baton to say, "Cap, don't tell me anything obvious because I know everything that's obvious. What certainly *isn't* obvious is what our leader really wants to do on the nuclear disarmament issue."

Weinberger nodded, his eyes wandering about the lavish jade ornamentation at the villa where Henry Luce had expected to rest his bones after his long and pre-eminent career as a publisher. The commanding single-story house had materialized notwithstanding Harry Luce's sudden death in 1967. "I told my architect," Mrs. Luce said to her guest, "'People will come and visit, but if Harry were here, they'd have made it a part of their working life to come to Honolulu. Now their visits will be to the widow, who is said to be herself entertaining, though less so than when she was married to the king of U.S. journalism.'"

"The widow known for her incisiveness and wit—"

"Yes, Cap. I don't deny that I like it that people seem to enjoy me—"

"Well, the President certainly enjoys you."

"That's true. Up to a point. Cap, did you ever meet Nancy Reagan's father, Dr. Loyal Davis?"

No. They hadn't met. But Weinberger knew of his reputation as a formidable medical doctor and man of affairs.

"In Phoenix we were neighbors. Harry died three years after we moved there. I used to tease Loyal that he was personally responsible for Harry Luce's death at such an early age."

"Do you really think that having lived to age sixty-eight, he had a convincing complaint against the doctors who looked after him?"

"No, you're right." Clare did not welcome conversational springboards that led immediately to questions about her own age. Harry Luce had been dead nineteen years, and Clare wasn't in a reproachful mood about his dying as she puffed on her cigarette and reminded herself, as she had put it to her stepson Hank Luce, that she intended to stop smoking sometime before her own death.

But now she wanted some big-think with the secretary of defense. "Everybody believes that our Ron is a big-time enthusiast for our nuclear weapons—"

He interrupted. "So you know about that. I'm not surprised."

"I've been hearing him on the subject dating back to the Phoenix days, when he and Nancy would visit her mother and stepfather. After all, Harry and I were neighbors."

Cap persisted. "As secretary of defense I live my life with the nuclear set. And you know something? Ronald Reagan detests that thing—the nuclear bomb—more than anyone I've ever dealt with."

"I know, I know. But maybe you and I are the only people who do know this. Which brings me to the point of the treaty. In terms of the here and now, what we have to do is keep things equal."

"If you mean, maintain a deterrent power, yes. Number-one priority."

"How are you going to do that in Europe with the Soviets' SS-20s?"

Weinberger's patience was wilting. "You know what the President plans to do. It's hardly a secret—any copyboy will tell you. The President proposes a nuclear ban. In bits and pieces. Objective Number 1, reduce the force level of Soviet weapons that can terrorize Europe—"

"By creating our own that can do the same thing to Mother Russia?"

"Well, yes. If we agreed to give up the development and deployment of intermediate-range missiles, there wouldn't be much point in Moscow continuing to develop them—"

"So, we hedge and counterhedge, and we're going to do what, end up with 10,000 nukes each?"

"I know what you're saying, Clare. And as a former member of the president's Foreign Intelligence Advisory Board, you know all the secrets. The secret that doesn't seem to arrest anybody's attention is that the President doesn't like a situation in which all life comes to rest on his ability to order a nuclear strike against— anybody. Mutual Assured Destruction. With our program of weapons reduction, we move conceptually away from MAD."

"Yes. Theoretically, if we reduced the inventory by 5 percent every year for twenty years, we'd have almost no nukes left."

"Yes. And that is the direction the President has agreed to go in his arms-reduction ideas. And he's willing to push his idea hard. But he doesn't see—and I don't either—what's going to alter the

Soviet determination to challenge the West and provoke disruption. So he goes through all the disarmament motions sincerely, and so here I am on one more international jaunt to push arms reduction in an Intermediate-Range Nuclear Forces treaty. INF. So—we'll get it. The treaty eliminates intermediate-range ground-based ballistic missiles *and* cruise missiles."

"Remind me. What is an intermediate range?"

"The treaty defines that as anywhere between three hundred and 3,400 miles."

"Enforced how?"

"Under the treaty, both nations are allowed to inspect each other's military installations."

"But there is only one thing that really lights up our leader's eyes. Star Wars."

"We don't call it that. We call it the Strategic Defense Initiative."

# Correspondence, 1986–1990

Dearest Nancy:

Well now, you certainly SCOOPED this journalist!
Got a phone call last night from Rosalyn Tureck,
just back from her tour of Europe, and she said, "I
guess you know I'm playing at the White House!"
Well, WFB did *not* know that the First lady had acted
on her servant's suggestion, and I am as excited as a
child. She is the most compelling performer, and I
guarantee you she will have the audience cheering.
Are you going to set it up in the fashion of
Horowitz? (who is a great admirer). Forty-five
minutes before dinner, that kind of thing? Whatever.
And how nice to do it on Bach's birthday: all the
Baroque-lovers will love you, I mean, love you more.
And oh yes, can I come?

Much love,
Bill

✄      ✄      ✄

February 14, 1986

Dearest Nancy:

The party was truly fine.[1] What you and Our Leader
referred to as the love in the room was there, and it
was palpable. The arrangements were memorable, and
you both looked stunning. I managed the entire
evening with only the single faux pas that I mistook
Audrey Six for Beverly Sills--not very bright, given
that the only person in the room I grew up with was
Audrey Cotter, as she was then called. She attended
the little school my father organized in our house.
It was very sweet of you to mention that I had come
all the way from Switzerland. Moreover, I was
ditched in Hartford, Connecticut, by the Concorde.
The lady on my left, a socialist peer, asked me, when
the captain gave the news of where we would come
down, "Where is Hartford?" I said I wasn't
absolutely sure, but I thought it was in Nova
Scotia.

An act of kindness? John Roche is Dean of the
Fletcher School of Diplomacy at Tufts. He was LBJ's
Henry Kissinger. He was--brace yourself--President
of Americans for Democratic Action! Then the
conversion began, and for ten years he wrote a
syndicated column so tough, so eloquent, so funny, we
ran it in *National Review* for the last three years.
He gave up the column, pleading academic overwork.
Now, finally, I hear from him. "The basic problem--
which has me checking my Army dog tag every so often
to recall my name--is that Connie is hospitalized
again." He then adds, "Connie and I are warm admirers

---

1. RR's 75th birthday party, at the White House.

of the President and Mrs. Reagan. Could you get us an inscribed photo?"

If anyone had told me a former head of ADA would ask for an inscribed photo of Ronald Reagan and Mrs. Reagan I would have questioned his sanity. But here is such a request--from the brightest man ever to serve in that role. It would be apt, if it isn't too much trouble, for the inscription to say something on the order of, "To John and Connie Roche: With high regard to a brilliant cold warrior," or something of the sort. Address: Office of the Dean, The Fletcher School of Law and Diplomacy, Tufts University, Medford, Mass.

Well, the only thing we missed on Friday was a visit with Rex. Loewy is here with us in Switzerland, and sends fraternal greetings. His boss sends love.

Bill

ร.       ร.       ร.

March 20, 1986

Dearest Nancy:

Well, now, that was one hell of a party. And the first of your State Dinners Pat and I have been to![2] Would you be kind enough to book us for the next sixteen?

Everything about it was perfect, including the expression on your face. Pat was quite irked when I told her--with that studied casualness which she so

_____

2. In honor of Prime Minister Brian Mulroney of Canada.

adores in me that one day she will divorce me over it--that the dessert you served was quite simply the best I have ever tasted. Do please bring that recipe to Casablanca.

I hope you were pleased by the performance of Rosalyn Tureck. She has had a lot of triumphs in her life, beginning as a child prodigy, and I have heard her perform more than twenty times, but I never saw her so exhilarated, and I think this showed up in her music. Really, dear N., you bring great radiance into everything you do. And I have to admit it, sigh, that the man you married is, well, worthy of you.

Pat joins in affectionate greetings to you both.

As ever,
Bill

＆　　　＆　　　＆

April 21, 1986

Dear Mr. President:

I enclose a column I wrote after hearing Henry Kissinger's unhappy story about his misrepresentation at the hands of ABC Television.[3] I called Bea (Mrs. Irving) Kristol, who was physically present, and she reassured me that Henry's account of what was said is exactly as I have written it. If you think of it, you might show my column to Nancy, as I know that Henry is anxious not to offend. A

---

3. See appendix, p. 256, "Understanding Reagan."

gentleman, someone wrote many years ago, gives
offense only intentionally . . .

It's been a month since I saw personally your
cheerful smile, or heard a good story from you, and
in turn I have been neglectful, though I have
performed my duties on the road. The spring break
away from Kabul is a great restorative. Although I
heave away pretty industriously--20 lectures,
April-May--I leave my duties in Afghanistan in good
hands, and you are not to reproach yourself for
permitting me this time away from the front lines.

On the road I am everywhere asked with some
impatience why our allies let us down last week.[4] God
knows there is no easy answer, but I do communicate
that the tremendous drop in tourist business to
Europe is probably not all motivated by fear of the
terrorists. Much of it is a gesture intended by
Americans--to convey their disgust. What would be
just fine is if traffic to England were heavy, but much
lighter to Spain and France. Although the polls are
interesting, divulging that sixty-one percent of
Frenchmen sympathized with what you did. And how do
you like the *New York Times* editorials? I swear,
they might have appeared in *National Review*, and
then you would need to go to an anniversary party of
the *NY Times*, and I could not stand that!

---

4. Reagan had ordered an air strike against Colonel Qaddafi's Libya in
retaliation for the bombing, by Libyan-directed terrorists, of a West Berlin
disco frequented by American servicemen. Margaret Thatcher had supported
Reagan and permitted F-111s to take off from British bases. The French and
Spanish governments had refused permission for the planes to overfly their
territory.

Give our love to your lady, and tell her we miss her. Back to the circuit. Among questions I am being asked are ones concerning my suggestion that some identifying mark be put on AIDS sufferers, to protect others, suggesting a tattoo on the upper arm, another on the buttocks. Got a certain amount of flak on that one, but they can't answer back when I say it ought to be a Gay Right not to be infected by someone already infected. Joe Sobran asked whether the rear tattoo might appropriately be the line from Dante, "Abandon hope, all ye who enter here!"

Bless you and, as always, Pat joins in affectionate regards to you both.

As ever,
Bill

ᡝ          ᡝ          ᡝ

August 21, 1986

Dear Mr. President:

Bill Rusher relayed your messages, and if my reply is a little blurred, that is the result of the almost inevitable diffusions that happen when a message goes from A to B to C.

You know me well enough to be confident that I hardly suspect your motives in selling the grain at a cut price to our friends in the Kremlin, and Bill tells me your purpose was to abort a comprehensive bill that hovered over Congress as a lowering threat. This was not made clear at the time, and neither *National Review* nor your other friends-- e.g., George Will; e.g., the government of Australia

(!)--picked it up. And even if you had made it clear, the symbolic impact of giving a special break to the Soviet Union strikes me as a heavy, heavy encumbrance on your unique role as keeper of the anti-Communist flame. I wish I could report better news from the anti-Communist community, but there has been deep dismay out here over that measure.

I was fascinated by the analysis Bill Rusher relayed respecting the ABM treaty and SDI.[5] I won't attempt to analyze it in any detail at second hand, but will leave you with only this thought. It is that, for the reasons you enunciated in March 1983, SDI is a strategic insight of unique moral dimensions. What is happening now, in our opinion, is a stigmatization of it by the usual people: It won't work. It's too expensive. It's too provocative. It is destabilizing. If I knew that five to seven years from now your hand would still be at the controls, I'd feel better about the airy talk of the past few weeks having to do with a five- to seven-year extension of ABM. But if the Congress, and the opinion-makers, and a large part of the public become convinced that SDI is in some way or another an obstacle to world peace, then it becomes stigmatized, and goes the way of the neutron bomb,

---

5. SDI, the Strategic Defense Initiative (dubbed by its opponents "Star Wars"), is the idea, embraced by Reagan, of replacing deterrence via Mutual Assured Destruction with anti-missile devices that could protect the target country. Opponents attempted to use the ABM (Anti-Ballistic Missile) treaty from the 1960s to stop SDI's development. . . . The MX was an American long-range ballistic missile developed in the 1970s as the answer to the Soviets' SS-18. It ran into a decade and a half of controversy over deployment methods. The neurton bomb was a tactical nuclear weapon designed to have low fallout.

MX: you know the route. I have done everything
except pray at night that you would cancel ABM, and
maybe now I'll do that too: my Big Bertha! But I am
of course glad to have your internal analysis.

Hope you got to see young Ron on his CBS interview.
As I wrote you both, he was really first-rate. Do me a
special favor and don't let on that I have taken a
couple of weeks away from my post at Kabul, but my
deputy there is a good man. He was for Reagan for
President in the middle forties when you were taking
on the Commies in Hollywood.

Pat joins in affectionate greetings to you and
Nancy.

As ever,
Bill

᠌᠌ᡶ᠆      ᡶ᠆      ᡶ᠆

April 5, 1987

Dear Mr. President:

Hi! I have neglected you in the mail for six weeks,
but you have been in my thoughts and you do a lot to
keep a columnist and editor busy: you are entitled to
put in for a royalty, come to think of it. I like best
what precedes any announcement of *anything* you do, to
wit: "In an effort to distract attention from the
Iranian question, President Reagan today (vetoed the
highway bill) (planned a visit with Canadian Prime
Minister Mulroney) (chopped wood) (took back the
Panama Canal) (played with Rex) (told Nancy he was
PO'd up to his keister with--pause!--why with me!)
(Dan Rather) (Sam Donaldson) (Tom Brokaw)."

You may remember that when you called me to ask if
I would see your friend Doug [Morrow], who is
organizing the brief television statements in
connection with the bicentenary (I am slated to go
with Tip O'Neill), you asked kindly how I was doing
with my new book,[6] and I told you I faced the problem
of constructing a narrative that would make the
reader sympathize with Blackford Oakes when, though
he had a radio in front of him, he did not use it to
warn the Secret Service that an attempt would be
made that morning on the life of President John F.
Kennedy. You wished me luck. Well, I did solve the
problem, but it required the threat of an
international nuclear war to do it.

Speaking of international nuclear wars, my own
reading of their improbability is the same as yours
when we first spoke on the subject twenty years ago:
that there is a direct correlation between their
improbability, and the absolute certainty that the
aggressor would find any such venture suicidal. I'm
not a bit sure I am enthusiastic about your INF
reductions, for reasons I will not burden you with.
But I do very much fear the crystallization of
national opinion around any offhand remarks by you
to the effect that nuclear weapons are obsolete,
which alas they are not. Politics has substantially
taken over our foreign policy, whether it is a
matter of the Contras or of the ABM treaty. And you
have the dreadful weight on your shoulders that
political platforms in 1987 and 1988 are going to
photograph you where you last took a step in the
direction of liberal cant--and go from there to the

---

6. *Mongoose, R.I.P.*

THE REAGAN I KNEW

left. There is nothing that can exorcise the formula
$E = mc^2$. The only thing we can do is to exorcise those
who deal lightly with that formula, which they will
exchange for human freedom any day. But then your
thoughts on this as on other matters are undoubtedly
known by our friends in the Kremlin, thanks to the
Marines.[7] Thank God we didn't send Sergeant Lonely
Heart, or whatever his name is, to Montezuma. If we
had, the capital of the U.S. would be Mexico City.

Great heavens, grandfather, what heavy thoughts
you have today. Well, it is Daylight Saving, and I
thought I would give my favorite president my
greetings. Give my love to our lady. Pat joins in
affectionate greetings.

As ever,
Bill

P.S. Just got your lovely note about mother's book.[8]
True, she never reminded us of one of King Henry
VIII's wives--but you make the nice point that if
she had been his first, she might also have been his
last. Swell of you to write.

---

7. Two Marine guards had been enticed by Soviet women with whom they were sexually involved into allowing KGB spies into the U.S. embassy in Moscow.

8. A memorial volume, *Aloïse Steiner Buckley, 1895–1985*, privately printed by the Buckley family.

May 5, 1987

Dear Bill:

Thank you for the early issue of *National Review*.[9]
I understand your "anxiety" and, yes, I have utmost
confidence in our personal relationship. I do,
however, believe the essays on possible arms
agreements with the Soviets overstate the risks and
understate my own awareness of the Soviet
conventional-weapon threat.

From the moment some six years ago (or thereabout)
when I went public with a zero-zero proposal on the
INF, I made it plain there would have to be a
redressing of the conventional-weapon imbalance.
Later, when I announced SDI, I made it plain it
should be based on the elimination of ballistic
missiles and that I favored sharing it with
everyone. I likened it to the outlawing of poison
gas after World War One and the fact that we all kept
our gas masks.

But closer to the point: my zero-zero proposal was
blasted far and wide, including by my then Secretary
of State, Al Haig. The theme was that zero-zero was
so drastic I had destroyed any chance of getting an
agreement with the Soviets. Well, here they are
proposing the same thing as if they thought of it
first. I have not changed my belief that we are
dealing with an "evil empire." In fact, I warned the
General Secretary in Reykjavik that his choice was
to join in arms reduction or face an arms race he
couldn't win.

---

9. The May 22 issue was devoted substantially to the Intermediate-Range
Nuclear Forces treaty. The cover line read: "Reagan's Suicide Pact."

Bill, if we can get an agreement on both long-range
and short-range missiles, in both of which the
Soviets have a sizeable edge, we'll still have more
than 4,000 nuclear warheads in Europe of the very
short range, including tactical battlefield weapons
and bombs. Any reduction of these would have to be
tied to conventional weapons on their side.

The most important thing is we intend to act with
our NATO allies at every step.

I know you realize this is a personal letter and
not a letter to the editor, and it comes with warmest
friendship. Love to Pat.

Sincerely,
Ron

✒        ✒        ✒

June 28, 1987

Dear Mr. President:

Thanks loads for your last letter on INF. I have
tried to incorporate into what I write the arguments
you make. Wish I could say you had convinced me, but
I remain so grateful that you haven't given the Erie
Canal to Panama that I need at least to keep that in
memory. We must agree to disagree--and to hope that
you are correct in your vaticinations (thought you'd
like that!). Johnny Carson pulled it on me last
week--a mistake! I even told him that vaticide was
the act of killing a prophet, and if he wanted to go
down as guilty of that crime, all he had to do was
kill me. And while I am at it, Nancy gave Pat (and
me) a great kick by saying that *you* got a kick from

my sailing book,[10] but that you could not make out
the inscription. It read, "To Ronald and Nancy
Reagan: From a devoted if refractory constituent."
Or something like that.

Please read the two attachments. One of them is a
copy of a letter you sent me a couple of years ago
about Bob Bork, the second a copy of the column I
sent out this morning.[11] What really did it was when
Senator Biden,[12] having at least eight times during
the past year announced that he would certainly
consider Judge Bork as qualified for a seat on the
Supreme Court, now announces that--well, er, ah, NOT
as a replacement for Judge Powell. If you are
qualified to sit on the Supreme Court, you are
qualified to sit on the Supreme Court. But I tell it
in my column I hope in a way that appeals to you. Our
friends over on the other side of the aisle are most
fearfully hypocritical. What they desire is a court
that will act as a supreme liberal legislature.
Don't let them have it! If you do, I shall be forced,
notwithstanding years of devoted service to you,
to--resign--my post as ambassador to Afghanistan.
Of course, I would do this tactfully.

You know, it's been a long while since we had some
time together, and maybe we should plan to do this,
say a short evening, or a long lunch. No special
hurry, but I see forces accumulating that for
personal and historical reasons you will want to

---

10. *Racing through Paradise*, an account of WFB & Friends' 1985 sail
across the Pacific, again on *Sealestial*.

11. See appendix, p. 258, "The Effort to Intimidate Reagan."

12. The Democrats had gained control of the Senate in 1986, and Joseph
Biden was now chairman of the Senate Judiciary Committee.

contend with. I don't pretend that my vision of them
is unique, but I am well trained, and back in 1961
you told me that in my book *Up from Liberalism* you
had got several useful insights. I may have one or
two left, and if so, I want you to have them. Perhaps
in August or September you and Nancy will find a hole
in your schedule. If you think of it, tell Nancy that
her Rex cushion[13] has given Pat more pleasure than
anything I have ever given her, save possibly my
eternal troth, though sometimes I wonder about that!
Bless you. Pat joins in affectionate greetings to
you both.

As ever,
Bill

Sunday,
October 18, 1987

Dear Mr. President:

Thanks a lot for your phone call. I digested your
complaints and intended to reply day before
yesterday, but your concern on that day, and mine
too, was for Nancy[14]; so I didn't engage in any
unnecessary distractions. Now, pray God, all is
well. Which means, I suppose, back to work.

Let me summarize my conclusions.

--I regret the tone and some of the references made
by Tom Bethell [in *National Review*]. You are aware,

---

13. A needlepoint cushion depicting the spaniel Rex.
14. Who had just undergone a mastectomy.

I know--you've told me so--that there are plenty of
people out there who, as you put it, think you have
joined the "galaxy" of détente-ists; that you seek--
again, as you put it--the "plaudits" of history,
maybe a Nobel Peace Prize, etc. As long as I am
editor of *NR*, which will be for another while,
inasmuch as we don't have a 22nd Amendment over in
these parts, *no personal criticism of this sort,
i.e., questioning your motives, will be published*. I
say this without any sense of professional
humiliation. My reasoning is as simple as that your
motives are beyond question. I know them to be what
they are from the record. And I know you as a friend
over twenty-five years. Enough said.

--Now this does not mean that our criticisms of the
pending treaty will discontinue.

We have a problem here. People are reading that
treaty differently when they talk to us than when
they talk to you. We have a great many contacts in
Europe, and they are telling us things they are not
telling you. Obviously you are aware that there are
Europeans who are unhappy, but you feel they are
unhappy out of ignorance. We are persuaded they
aren't: that they are unhappy because they are
afraid of the long-term consequences of the treaty.

This letter isn't a paper presenting the other
side, so let me just give you two or three
propositions, succinctly put:

1. SDI is not going to survive merely because you
are in favor of it. Unhappily, it is, in my judgment,
going to be spiked by Congress. Congress will be
reacting to pressure initiated by the Soviet Union,
played through its worldwide echo chambers, on into
American liberalism. Congress will starve SDI to

death after you have left the White House. The
pressure of the Soviet Union is in part generated by
the success of their recent diplomatic
maneuverings.

2. The mere existence of Western nuclear firepower
to defend West Germany against a nuclear ultimatum
doesn't argue that--*when you are no longer president*--
that firepower will be leveled right at the Kremlin
with the simple warning: Cut it out. The Europeans I
correspond with believe that the removal of land-
based missiles that could reach Soviet territory from
Western Europe will persuade the Soviet Union that,
under an indecisive president, they can safely
proceed on the assumption that no American President
is going to commit nuclear forces to stop a Soviet
blitzkrieg. What would we actually do if they showed
up with an SS—20 at the Brandenburg Gate?

3. It isn't only the far right that is made
unhappy by present plans. Bernard Rogers is hardly a
member of the jerk-right. Or Jeane Kirkpatrick. Or
Henry Kissinger. Or Bill Hyland. Or Al Haig. They
join the editors of *NR* in fearing the consequences
of what is going on--primarily in a post-Reagan age.

4. I know what you mean about the nuclear age, but
in fact we owe the liberty of most of those who are
free to the existence of nuclear power. And almost
certainly I owe my own life to it, having been a
nubile 2nd lieutenant in the infantry at the time of
Hiroshima. Seventy-five million people were killed
on earth, violently, during this century, before the
bomb was discovered that has thus far killed one
hundred thousand.

\#

There. You know I could go on--and I will go on, in
*NR* and in my column and speeches. But never with a
hint of disrespect for a man I know well and trust
totally. Besides, no one sees any particular threat
to Casablanca, and isn't that the pre-eminent point?

Pat joins me in affectionate greetings to you and
Nancy, who is in our prayers.

> Yours ever,
> Bill

ะะ              ะะ              ะะ

> Sunday,
> January 24, 1988

Dear Mr. President:

It was super lunching with you the other day in
your little querencia. I was a little alarmed that
you referred to me as your ambassador in front of the
photographer. Should we run a special security check
on him? But I'm sure he will be quiet.

Thanks for the info on so many subjects. Was
fascinated by what you told me about the damage to
one's acting career that long service as a union
president could do to you. Hadn't heard that before,
but it makes sense. On the matter of INF, we shall
have to agree to disagree. Damn I wish I could be on
your side on that one. Haven't had a significant
difference with you since Panama Canal. Which
reminds me, events of the past few weeks may suggest
that that little loophole in the treaty will be
useful to us.[15]

Am upset about the Deaver business.[16] No doubt you saw Safire, and of course the *Wash. Times* has been full of it. *National Review* has remained silent, as I have. If you and/or Nancy has a nifty way of handling it, ask her kindly to give me a buzz. I hate like hell to hit Mike when he's down,[17] but damn, I wish he hadn't written so provocatively. I simply don't understand friends who turn around and divulge confidences.

I didn't tell you I am going to write a play in February? Yes: *Stained Glass* (maybe you read the novel--it was the one that got the American Book Award). After you've done repealing the 22nd Amendment, if you're looking around for a taste of the old profession, merely call

                   Your devoted friend,
                   Bill

      ✍        ✍        ✍

---

15. Against a background of unrest in Panama, the U.S. Justice Department was investigating General Manuel Antonio Noriega—successor to General Torrijos—on charges of abetting the international drug trade. The "loophole" was the provision that the United States has the right to intervene militarily if necessary to keep the canal open.

16. Word was getting out about the contents of Deaver's forthcoming book, *Behind the Scenes: In Which the Author Talks about Ronald and Nancy Reagan . . . and Himself.* Deaver claimed that he and Mrs. Reagan had frequently collaborated to persuade President Reagan to soften an overly conservative stand.

17. Meanwhile, Deaver had been convicted for perjury in connection with his lobbying activities after he left the administration.

February 1, 1988

Dear Bill:

Don't worry about the photographer, I've had him shot.

I still think we are on solid ground on the INF Treaty based on our verification provisions and on the fact that Gorby knows what our response to cheating would be--it's spelled Pershing.

Bill, hold your fire on Deaver. Our information is that some of the usual press editing of his answers in an interview was slanted. We'll have to wait until we see his book.

We are both excited about your new undertaking, and of course we will both be at liberty in the near future. Is there a juvenile character and an ingénue contemplated in your script--important roles of course? We'll be waiting for opening night and the movie version.

Nancy sends her love--so do I.

Sincerely,
Ron

✎       ✎       ✎

November 13, 1988

Dear Mr. President and Nancy:

I address you jointly because this is in an important respect a personal letter, i.e., it focuses on the esteem in which Ronald Reagan is held by his countrymen. Nobody has invested more devoted attention to that esteem than you, dear Nancy, and

don't think this escapes me when I am left alone,
sighing in Casablanca!

My advice, given to you for professional and
personal reasons, is that you grant a pardon to
Poindexter (and, of course, North).[18]

I think it important for the future of effective
government because inherent in the prosecution at
least of Poindexter is an effort to criminalize
political activity. I don't plan to be president,
but George is practically there. He and his
successors would, in my estimation, be damaged by
a prosecutorial act which if it is to succeed has
inevitably to probe and condemn a relationship
that, in order to be effective, has got to be
protected. The danger if you wait to see what it is
the prosecutors have come up with and then decide
whether he should be pardoned is that that day
will come way after you have left the White House.
It is you Poindexter sought to serve, not George
Bush. That is one aspect of the moral question;
and therefore it is you, in my judgment, who
should exercise your undisputed authority in this
matter.

I took the liberty of telephoning Bill Smith to
confide to him my feelings in the matter. He
authorized me to tell you that he has zero moral

---

18. Rear Admiral John Poindexter and Lieutenant Colonel Oliver North
had both been indicted for their role in the Iran-Contra affair. This had
evolved from the fact that Congress had been on again, off again, sometimes
agreeing to Reagan's requests to fund the anti-Communist Contras in
Nicaragua, then turning around and denying funding. As a result, some
members of the Reagan administration had devised a scheme to get money
for the Contras while bolstering Iranians whom they perceived as moderate.

objections to your issuing a pardon. He has more to
say that is interesting, in the event you feel like
calling him.

It is certainly true that if you now have, let us
say, 60 units of esteem, after pardoning Poindexter
you would have 57 units of esteem. But if the
prosecution goes forward, inevitably (I should
judge) your professional detractors would labor to
lower your esteem as the result of the material that
is spread out before the jury. And your esteem would
stand a chance of reducing to below 57—as also that
of your successor. I don't know whether George has
any feelings on the subject and obviously I shan't
inquire, but it is a factor you no doubt bear in
mind.

And then there is the crowning consideration. It
is inconceivable that the defense lawyers of
Poindexter and North will fail to call you to the
stand, and no lawyer I have spoken with doubts that
you would need to go and give testimony. In order to
do this, you will be instrumental in exposing to
public view the mechanisms by which the United
States protects its vital interests. What the Left
in America will do with this is absolutely
unthinkable.

I met Poindexter only once: I can't remember
whether it was at your birthday party, or at the
party for Mr. Mulroney. We exchanged only a word or
two, so that I have no personal interest in the
matter, save as we are all a little bit involved in
mankind and I have the feeling that he is alone,
indigent, and a patriot.

So there you both have it. I don't intend to write
publicly about this; though if you did in fact

extend the pardon, I would then write boisterously to commend you for doing the right thing.

Other than to re-suggest that you give a Medal of Freedom to Robert Bork, I have no further instructions for today.

Pat joins me in affectionate greetings to you both.

As ever,
Bill


&#8266;    &#8266;    &#8266;


November 23, 1988

Dear Nancy:

What fun it was to be with you for an hour.[19] And how thoughtful and generous of you to select me as your dinner partner. Some of the ground we traversed was a little saddening, a little melancholy. . . . But you looked so perfect, and your toast was so warm. I love Barbara, but the White House won't be the same without you. I'll call you before we go away for Xmas. Come to think of it, I'll call you way before that! Pat joins in sending love,

Bill


&#8266;    &#8266;    &#8266;


---

19. At a dinner for President Reagan in Washington hosted by Kay Graham, owner of the *Washington Post*.

January 31, 1989

Bill, dear--

Thanks for sending the column, which I hadn't
seen.[20] It was so nice about both of us and we both
appreciate it more than you know.

I was so happy you and Pat were there for the
"portrait diaries"--you'll be glad to know Ronnie's
is being redone! I don't know how that went so wrong,
but it did--so it will be a while until they're hung.
We wanted to display them the next day. We miss you
and Pat terribly--you're going to have to come West
often--okay?

Love and Xs
Nancy

🖎          🖎          🖎

February 16, 1989

Dear Bill:

I'm honored by your invitation to be a member of
*National Review*'s Board of Directors and say yes if
you mean it about probable non-attendance at
meetings. My so-called retirement has taken on a kind
of frantic or frenetic activity. First on the
schedule are the two books I've signed up for and have
not as yet put pen to paper for even one word. So can
I accept with the promise you so generously offered?

You realize, of course, that your eight years of
service in Kabul give you the title of Ambassador

---

20. See appendix, p. 260, "A Farewell to the Reagans."

for life. Just think of the doors such a title might
open! And, of course, you can claim credit for the
Soviet withdrawal from Kabul.

Nancy sends her love and from both of us to Pat.

Sincerely,
Ron

🙠          🙠          🙠


February 14, 1990

Dear Mr. President:

Before I forget, would you please ask your wife if
she will be my Valentine? I mean, before I read Kitty
Kelley's book. (Kelley sent me a copy of her last
letter to Nancy asking for an interview, repeating
the request of me. I have only said No three times.
Just Say No.) Where was I?

Yes, October 5. I was going to wait until the
spring to ask you to be our guest of honor at the
35th anniversary celebration of *National Review*.
And then the following coincidence: Our assistant
business manager was at the Waldorf to sign the final
contract for our engagement when she learned that
you were going to give a speech that same day at
lunch for Citicorp! So I am acting with the speed of
light, for which I and Superman are renowned--lest
you are approached by some Philistine group to
address them that night, rather than us.

It will be a very special night for me, as I shall
retire effective the following issue of the magazine
as CEO of *National Review*. I thought of pressing for
a repeal of the 22nd Amendment, but decided finally

to yield to the younger generation. On the other
hand, I might decide to run for president, and would
appreciate your advice on that subject.

But do please confirm that *National Review*'s Man of
the Decade will be with us, addressing the entire
world, and also his fellow directors.

Pat joins in affectionate greetings to you both.

As always,
Bill

P.S. As you know, we follow the tradition that
people are invited by a committee of Friends of
*National Review* to our banquets. They are, always, a
man of affairs, an academic, and a politician. This
year these will be Bill Simon, Milton Friedman, and
Henry Hyde.

ɤ.       ɤ.       ɤ.

April 2, 1990

Dear Mr. President:

It is heartbreaking news that you won't be able to
attend our 35th, and my final, Anniversary Dinner. I
retaliate by declining to repeal the 22nd Amendment.
It simply won't be, without you, what it might have
been. But, of course, I understand. . . .

Mike Weiner, who is president of Microlytics,
Inc., a division of Xerox (address: One Tobey
Village Office Park, Pittsford, NY 14534) is an old
epistolary friend who is engaged in great romantic
adventures in the computer world. They have just
developed an extraordinary pocket Bible. You can find

any passage in the entire Bible by merely tapping
out one key word and pushing FIND. It is truly
remarkable. He has asked me to serve as a conduit,
Bible to you: which I consented to do
notwithstanding your unavailability on October 5.
You will find it infinitely diverting and rewarding. I
know he would appreciate a brief acknowledgment.

Had a long and not reassuring conversation with
Nancy from Switzerland. I do desperately hope she
accepts history as your great vindicator and ceases
to be tormented by the little scorpions who will
never forgive you your success in office.

Pat joins in affectionate greetings.

As ever,
Bill

❦    ❦    ❦

April 6, 1990

Dear Bill,

Thanks for delivering the electronic Bible. It has
only just arrived. I'm still trying to figure out
whether I'm up to translating the instructions or
not. However I'm fascinated with it and wonder how
much further technology can take us. I'm writing a
thank you to Mike Weiner but again thanks to you.
It's been "a long time between drinks"--have to do
something about that. Nancy sends her love and from
both of us to Pat.

I'm really up to my limit on the mashed potato
circuit. If this is retirement I'd rather go back to
work.

Again thanks and all the best.

Ron

🖎    🖎    🖎

May 29, 1990

Dear Mr. President:

It was great to speak with you, but sad to learn
that you have been ill. I hope by now the docs are
letting you eat hazel nuts and jelly beans. . . . Your
recalling the source of the trouble reminded me of
the letter Evelyn Waugh wrote Nancy Mitford after
reading a report in the *Times* that morning. "The
paper advises that the doctors removed a benign
tumor from Randolph Churchill yesterday. Leave it to
science to find and remove the only part of Randolph
that was benign."

Great on the book.[21] You will send me the name of
the gentleman at the publisher, and I'll arrange
with Warren Steibel for a *Firing Line*. And don't
forget, you promise this time not to give away
another of our canals.

Give my love to Nancy. Will give her a buzz in the
next week or so, now that I know you are safely in
this country for a few weeks.

Pat joins in affectionate greetings to you both.

As ever,
Bill

---

21. Reagan's autobiography was about to be published.

# 19

# Final Meeting

The last time Reagan and I met was in Los Angeles, in October of 1990. He had agreed to do a *Firing Line* episode focusing on his newly published autobiography, *An American Life*. I was taken to his office, high in one of those officious buildings on the west side of town. My camera crew had arrived and set up. Reagan was taking the last minute before the taping, seated in his desk chair, with a cup of tea. He greeted me warmly, said a word or two about his book plans, then suddenly thrust his cup of tea toward me.

"Stick your finger in this."

"*What?*"

"Yeah. Go ahead."

I raised my index finger, put it in the tea, and withdrew it quickly from the scalding liquid.

"Now, watch this." Reagan lifted the cup and took a swallow from it. "See? The tolerance of your mouth tissues is infinitely greater than that of your hand!"

I expressed the surprise I felt.

"You know who taught me that? It was Frank Sinatra."

❧        ❧        ❧

The program was not memorable—among other things, the hearing problem that had bothered him for some time was getting worse—though Reagan reacted as the consummate performer when the opportunity arose:

REAGAN: . . . And so this economic program that we put into effect— Incidentally, I knew it was succeeding when they stopped calling it Reaganomics. . . . But the fact is that for eight years we had the longest and biggest economic recovery and economic growth in our entire history.

BUCKLEY: There is a school of constitutional thought that the line-item veto inheres in presidential prerogatives as specified in the Constitution. Were you ever tempted to try that out by vetoing a part of a bill to see whether the Supreme Court would sustain you?

REAGAN: Well, I had suggested such a thing, but nobody ever thought that it was worth while doing. I had to veto the whole thing or else, and it is— Well, let me just point out a contrast. As governor of California for eight years, having that, I used the line-item veto 943 times.

BUCKLEY: And you were never overruled.

REAGAN: I was never overruled once, even though the legislature that had sent me the things that I line-item vetoed— It took a two-thirds majority of them to send it to me. It only took two-thirds to override my veto, but they never could get the two-thirds when they had to vote on an item standing out there all by itself where the people could see it. When they could bury it in a package, well then they would try.

REAGAN: . . . I have told him [Gorbachev] that I would advocate making that information [about SDI] open to the world.

BUCKLEY: Well, you always have.

REAGAN: Yes. In return for all of us destroying our nuclear weapons. But I said the reason then for having it is, and I used the example of World War I. I said, you know, all the nations after World War I met and outlawed poison gas, but we all kept our gas masks. And I said, Who can say that down the way someday there won't be another Hitler, there won't be another madman that could use the knowledge of how to make weapons and blackmail the earth?

BUCKLEY: To what extent do you continue to believe that our country is providentially blessed and guided?

REAGAN: Bill, you can call this mysticism, if you will. I have always had a feeling, a belief, that this continent was placed here between the two great oceans to be found by people from wherever in the world who had an extra ounce of desire for freedom and an extra ounce of courage in order to pick up and leave friends and countrymen and so forth and come to this country. . . .

There is a man who wrote me a letter just before I left office, and I have to share it with you. This letter, just briefly—

BUCKLEY: You have 10 seconds.

REAGAN: Let me just say, he said, "You can go to live in France, but you can't become a Frenchman. You can go to live in Italy, but you can't become an Italian." And he cited all of them, Japan, Turkey, all these. But he said, "Anyone, from any corner of the earth, can come to America and become an American."

BUCKLEY: Thank you, Mr. President.

I remember reading years later in Edmund Morris's *Dutch* repeated references to Morris's having crossed Reagan's path over several years when Reagan simply forgot who he, his chosen biographer, was. The implication was that the dissolution we all by then knew about had set in much earlier than anyone had guessed.

Actually, I had had, many years earlier, an experience that put this in a different perspective. It was 1967, and Reagan was doing a Chubb Fellow visit to Yale. The tradition is a cocktail party/dinner on Day 1. On Day 2, a formal address, followed by a reception at the host college (Timothy Dwight), the guest of honor standing, the college master and a personal friend standing by his side, students and faculty filing by to shake the guest's hand. I would have the same experience with Reagan two or three times again in similar circumstances, recalling it especially during a hand-shaking sequence at a political convention and at a *National Review* banquet.

What happened was that at a certain moment a faintly detectable glaze fell over his eyes. *Nothing else was noticeable.* His pleasantries were spontaneous, his head often bowed slightly to catch every word. But when the glaze set in, whatever faculty it is that informs you on the matter of who it is you are talking to, in Reagan, simply cut out.

He had invited me to stand by his side, as an old friend who had furnished the pheasant for the dinner the night before. Nancy, at the other end of the room, was doing her own socializing.

About the twenty-third guest came by, and I knew that Reagan was no longer distinguishing them.

Then an electric moment. A particular guest had grabbed Reagan's hand firmly and was leaning just slightly toward him, a summons to that extra little intimacy often seen on receiving lines.

But while Reagan's smile was warm, his hand actively engaged in the guest's hand, suddenly the guest withdrew his hand. "Ronnie," he said, in a voice just a little strained. "This is me. George Bush." The glaze lifted, and there was some lively patter between the Chubb Fellow who thirteen years later would become president and the man who would become his vice president and successor.

❧       ❧       ❧

The *Firing Line* taping was done, and I was led down, with Reagan, to his sedan, en route to his home on a neighboring hill, to take lunch.

Riding in a sedan instead of a limousine must have been hard to get used to for someone who had just spent eight years in the White House after eight years as governor of California. Reagan was big, and so am I, so that our knees were touching the back of the front seat. This was not topped by any partition at all to separate us from the driver, who was black, and the Secret Service agent who sat alongside him.

"Well, what do you think? It went okay?"

I reassured him, but decided to enter a single criticism.

In his book, Reagan recalled that Supreme Court Justice Thurgood Marshall had labeled President Reagan the most racist president since Herbert Hoover. Reagan wrote that he was astonished by this and wounded. So Reagan arranged a meeting with Marshall. This is what he said about it in his memoirs: "We spoke for an hour or so upstairs in the family quarters, and I literally told him my life story—how Jack and Nelle had raised me from the time I was a child to believe racial and religious discrimination was the worst sin in the world, how I'd experienced some of it as the son of an Irish Catholic in a Protestant town; how as a sports announcer I'd been among the first in the country to campaign for integration of professional baseball; how I'd tried as governor to open up opportunities for blacks. That night, I think I made a friend." I told him I had found this story a bit defensive.

Reagan wanted to give me a fuller explanation, but there was the problem of the black driver. Reagan lifted a pencil from his pocket and pointed it toward the driver. "You see, Bill, my family was *always* opposed to any discrimination against"—he jabbed the pencil in the direction of the driver. Reagan didn't want even to mention the race-word, within the hearing of his black chauffeur.

At lunch there was only Nancy and Ron Jr. After a few minutes it became plain that conversation was not expected at a pitch high enough to guarantee his hearing of it and participation in it. From time to time he would initiate a talking point, and the conversation would be general. But soon his voice quieted, and his attention was paid to the food, not to whatever was on the mind of his wife, son, and old friend.

# Correspondence, 1990–2005

*"I recall that Henry Mencken described an introduction to him on a celebratory occasion as having evoked 'a full moon, the setting sun, and the aurora borealis.' In this perspective, if all the generous things Mark Burson has said really belong to me, how am I expected even to intimate the achievements of Ronald Reagan? Well, I can do that, really, in one sentence.*

*"He succeeded in getting Nancy Reagan to marry him.*

*"The country is familiar with the legend of Nancy, familiar with her accomplishments as companion, aide, monitor, wife, and lover. There was never anyone who more devotedly served a husband. She has renewed for us all the meaning of the pledge to stand by in sickness and in health."*

—From the keynote address at a symposium in honor of
Ronald Reagan's eighty-eighth birthday, at the Ronald
Reagan Library and Museum, Simi Valley, California,
February 4, 1999

❧        ❧        ❧

September 25, 1990

Dear Bill,

I've been on the go for a while (Germany, Poland, Russia, and Rome)--there, that's my alibi for not answering your letter of Sept. 7. Thanks for the clipping about Alden Whitman.[1] I haven't shed a single tear.

The trip was great, and Americans are popular in every country we visited. The people in the street openly declare the U.S. is responsible for all the improvements and for what appears to be a widespread movement toward our way of life. We attended church in Leningrad. The church was packed with more than 1,000 people. Religion is openly discussed wherever you go.

Well, Nancy sends her love and from both of us to Pat.

Ron

≈        ≈        ≈

April 18, 1991

Dear Nancy:

I talked yesterday with our favorite president, and he told me you were feeling a little blue. And why not? It hurts that anyone, even a certified

---

1. The clipping was the notice of Whitman's death. Several years earlier, Whitman, the *New York Times's* chief obiturist, had written that "President Reagan is Bringing fascism to America as certainly as Mussolini did to Italy." In 1956, under questioning from the Senate Internal Security Subcommittee, Whitman admitted that he had been a member of the Communist Party for thirteen years.

viper, should have written such stuff.[2] Every now and again I read, in a biography or even in an autobiography, that So & So after a while ceased to be affected by criticism, never mind how unmerited. It is not so, at least not in my experience. I have published 32 books, and I'd have bet everything, after the first twenty, that there remained no unspoken calumny about me. Well, it isn't true. They keep coming. What is true is that they do continue to wound. I guess it's fair to say that I get over it much quicker than I did when I was 24 (want to see my birth certificate?): but it still stings, and so I know what pain you are going through. I have the book, trying to decide whether to write publicly about it beyond the column you so kindly acknowledged.[3] There are three references to me. The accurate one is that I attended the party you gave for the Prince of Wales. Somehow, she got that straight. The other two are inaccurate. You and Ron Sr. and Jr. came not to *my* family estate in Sharon, but to my mother's, for Thanksgiving. . . . I had exactly nothing to do with little Ron's getting into Yale. . . . And what she contrives to make appear as an interview with her, she pulled out of my book *Cruising Speed*, and of course put her own spin on it. Speaking of sensitivity, I like to think she has a trace of it, in which event she can feel something of the contempt civilized people have for her. As far

---

2. Best-selling sleaze-monger Kitty Kelley had just published *Nancy Reagan: The Unauthorized Biography*, 640 pages of allegations that Mrs. Reagan was an abusive mother, an unfaithful wife, and a woman so credulous as to be guided by astrology.

3. See appendix, p. 263, "The Democrats Win with a Sweep."

as I am concerned, I can only remember one kindness
after another, by you, for me, for Pat. And your
devotion to your mother was as exemplary as any I
have ever known, from offspring to parent. You have
had a wonderful life, prevailing over many sorrows.
This is just one more, but for every such sorrow,
there will be, I know, a compensating joy, cf. the
Christian religion, which gives us, always, life and
hope. With love,

Bill

꒦      ꒦      ꒦

May 7, 1991

Dear Bill,

Our heartfelt thanks for the tape you sent.[4] Nancy
and I played it last night and enjoyed it
tremendously. Of course there was a bit of regret
that someone was stepping down. We'll miss you.
Looking back I now can see you played a part in my
becoming a Republican. Again thank you. Nancy sends
her love & from both of us to Pat.

Ron

꒦      ꒦      ꒦

---

4. Of *National Review*'s 35th Anniversary party.

August 19, 1991

Dear Bill:

Thank you for your note of August 10th. I'm glad to see you left Afghanistan free of the Soviets when you departed. (Do you think we could send you to Cuba next?)

With regard to the paragraph you stopped in *National Review*, I'm very glad you did. As a friend I've got to tell you I am damn mad about the version of events that some *unnamed* source keeps putting out about the Library Board.

The truth is that no one was ousted from the Library Board. As the by-laws have always stated, Trustees will serve six-year terms. Ed Meese, Bill Clark, and Marty Anderson were among the first groups of Trustees I appointed in 1985. In fact, they drafted the by-laws. . . .

I'm sorry too I missed the Grove this year. You know for my eight-year term on the eastern front, I just couldn't go. Since I've been back in Los Angeles I've made it to the Grove the past two years, but this year it didn't work out on the schedule.

Nancy told me of your nice call on her birthday. Both of us are really looking forward to visiting Morocco. From what we've heard, some places there haven't changed in a thousand years. (Which should make me feel right at home!)

Nancy joins me in sending our best to you and Pat. We look forward to seeing you soon.

Sincerely,
Ron

October 18, 1991

Dear Stranger:

Well now, are you back from Casablanca? Do you think
it will do for us? . . . Has been decades since we
talked, and the loss is mine. Have been furiously
busy, got back from England, where the National
Review Institute sponsored a wonderful weekend
seminar with Mrs. Thatcher as m/c. Would you believe
it, one of our guests turned to her on Saturday and
said he was going to give one hundred thousand bucks
to the Thatcher Institute. Then the next day he turned
to her and said, "Since today is your birthday, I am
going to make that TWO hundred thousand dollars."
Dear Nancy, my birthday is on Nov 24, would you please
give me two hundred thousand dollars? I promise not to
dribble it away. . . . I was in England during the
Clarence Thomas do. God! I hope you saw the amusing
David Barry column. In case you didn't, I enclose a
copy. We are off tomorrow to the Caribbean for a week
on a sailboat, one of those huge Club Med things. But
Van is a Director of Club Med and promises I won't die
of boredom. How could I, am finishing a 35,000-word
essay on anti-Semitism, which will run in the first
issue of *NR* in December. Full of interesting stuff,
you bet. And guess what I'll be doing at noon Nov
18?????? Receiving the Medal of Freedom at the WH. I
will whisper to the doorkeepers that I am a SPECIAL
friend and fan of Nancy Reagan, and I know they will
take good care of me. Pat joins in affectionate
greetings to you and our favorite President.

Love,
Bill

༄         ༄         ༄

May 15, 1992

Dear Mr. President and Nancy:

I so much appreciated your calling me in New York.
I read in the papers that one day very soon when
that happens a beeper will ring in my pocket in
Grand Rapids (where I was), and then with great
sangfroid, I shall leave the lectern, saying,
Excuse me, ladies and gentlemen, but you know, I
*cannot* keep Mrs. Reagan and the President waiting
on the phone.

I hope you had a pleasant time in New York. I have
been all over the place, preaching the word of the
Lord and of our penultimate President. Between thee
and me, I don't think Pat Buchanan has done a very
convincing job. I see that in New Hampshire, to
which he repaired in order to reorient the GOP "in
the direction Ronald Reagan took it," he came out
(a) for an increase in unemployment benefits; (b) for
the elimination of all aid to every country abroad
(total: $13 billion); (c) for eliminating the
National Endowment for the Arts (total: $312
million); and (d) for eliminating one half the raise
Congress gave itself (total: $9 million). The sum of
all of this would diminish the federal budget by 0.9
percent. Oh dear.

But why are we talking about world affairs? It has
been much too long since we visited, and I'm sorry
you didn't see Pat in New York, but she loved
talking with you. I am off to Korea and Taiwan and
Hong Kong, back on June 2; then ten days in Greece at

the end of the month; then back to my book.[5] In
between, I have to play the D Minor Bach Concerto
with a symphony orchestra. Please remember, on the
night of June 13, to pray for me, and also for the
poor people in Poughkeepsie, New York, who have to
listen to me.

Had a very chirpy letter from young Ron, who liked
my book *WindFall*. No doubt he was influenced to do so
by the blurb on the back jacket from my Favorite
President. Trust you are both thriving and that
we'll visit soon. Meanwhile Pat joins me in
affectionate greetings to you both.

> As ever,
> Bill

❧          ❧          ❧

> March 19, 1994
> CONFIDENTIAL

Dear Mr. President:

This is a VERY important letter, for us and, I
hope, for you. The idea traces to a conversation
with Rush Limbaugh in January.

We decided that what the United States needs above
all things in life is a monster demonstration of the
admiration and affection so many of us feel for--you.
We spent some time deliberating whether the affair
should be held in New York or in Washington, and

---

5. *In Search of Anti-Semitism*, an expansion to book length of the essay
mentioned above.

concluded that Washington was the appropriate
locale. It is there that you entered history and
officiated over the best years America has had in my
lifetime.

So: Should it be outdoors or indoors? We decided
indoors, for the simple reason that it is less easy
for the professional distracters to get in the way.
There is no place in Washington big enough for the
assembly Rush is absolutely confident he can gather
together. But what used to be called the Capital
Center (over which you have several times presided),
now called the U.S. Air Arena, holds eighteen
thousand people. It will be overflowing.

Date? We gave a lot of thought to this, through
which I won't bother to take you. But the consensus
was: Labor Day Sunday, September 4. Perfect in terms
of a day off before and after the event. And then we
are only eight weeks before a national election in
which we have a shot at the Senate. Your tribute
could ignite the old fires, which have been
substantially out since the day you left office. We'd
have some film clips of senators running for
election, paying tributes to you.

Time? Late afternoon or early evening.

The sponsors would be Rush, plus *National Review*,
and the Media Research Center in Washington,
presided over by my nephew Brent Bozell. The
physical arrangements and coordination are a
monstrous job, but he is super-able.

Program? Leave it to us. Rush and I spoke about a
few live testimonials, from such as Bob Hope and
Chuck Heston and Johnny Carson, a little music, a lot
of (dare I?) gaiety--and an acknowledgment from you.
The proceeds of the event? To the Reagan Library.

Well, what do you say, pal?[6] We want all the world to know how brightly you continue to shine in our memory.

Apart from my service to you in Afghanistan, I deem this the most important political enterprise of the age.

Pat joins in affectionate greetings to you both.

As ever,
Bill

cc: R. Limbaugh
    B. Bozell

꙳       ꙳       ꙳

Dictated in Switzerland
Transcribed in New York
February 13, 1996

Dearest Nancy:

Called you last week, but you were out of town until Friday. The person who answered the phone had an accent and I thought her Mexican so I tried out a little Spanish on her but she stuck to English, and had a hard time writing my complicated last name! She said you'd be back Friday and she would give you the message. We are in Switzerland for the annual book-writing[7] and just wondering how you are doing. The clouds seems to be darkening, in Russia, in

---

6. Instead of a letter from President Reagan, WFB received a phone call from Mrs. Reagan, saying, "Ronnie is simply not up to it." Eight months later Reagan wrote his letter to the American people announcing his withdrawal from public life.

7. *Nearer, My God: An Autobiography of Faith.*

China, in North Korea. And the incumbent in the White House seems awfully certain he will stay there a while. Did you see Christopher's hilarious page on Hillary in *The New Yorker*? If you haven't, and want a copy, call Frances Bronson in my office. Pat joins me in much love.

As always,
Bill

ঙ৲        ঙ৲        ঙ৲

April 12, 1998

Dear Nancy:

It was fine talking with you. Was in Palm Springs overnight for a debate, part of a series of speakers, the first of whom was Margaret Thatcher. She praised robustly, I was told, the achievements of Our Favorite President. By contrast, Speaker #3 was Vincent Bugliosi (the prosecutor), who slighted RR, causing some people actually to leave the hall during the question period. I arrived the next day. . . . Henry Kissinger greeted me with a chapter from his new book about Nixon. It is marvelously accomplished, the analysis of Nixon's personality, his suicidal temptations. The current issue of *Time* Mag has pieces on illustrious gentry of the century (including one by me on Pope JP), and Edmund Morris's on Teddy Roosevelt is terrific. They say his big book[8] will be out this fall. I will believe it when I see it. (Peggy Noonan did RR, appropriately worshipful.) Speaking of seeing people, when do I

---

8. *Dutch: A Memoir of Ronald Reagan.*

get to see you? Much love, in which my absent wife
(Nassau) joins--we spoke this morning.

Bill


ह.      ह.      ह.


August 15, 2005

Love of my life!!

Thanks tons for your note, which reminded me of my
sad dereliction trying to get through to you from
Corsica.[9] No wonder Napoleon lost! Now, the BIG news.
I must be in L.A. Saturday evening September 17.
Would you believe it, a fundraiser apropos of
*National Review*'s 50th anniversary. If only our
favorite president might have been there! Without
him the journal would not have made it, nor would the
country. I can, by going early, get to L.A. in time
to have lunch with you. Okay? I know you like the
Beverly Wilshire. (Was that where we had dinner? And
where Patti was married?) I could meet you there or
pick you up. Is 1:15 okay? So dying to see you. I
have my one week's sailing vacation this week so
won't be near a handy phone. I might ask Frances
Bronson to call to clear the date: Lunch, September
17th, 1:15, Beverly Wilshire (or anywhere else you
prefer). What shall I bring you? An artist's sketch
of the new Mt. Rushmore? XXXB

---

9. The Buckleys were sailing with friends in the Mediterranean in early
July, and WFB was unable to get a phone connection to reach Mrs. Reagan
on the day of her birthday and his and Pat's wedding anniversary.

# 20

# Coda

I cannot do better, in summing up the Reagan years, than to repeat what I said in my first speech of the 1990s.

On traversing New Year's Eve—I told the audience in Florida—and thinking back on the decade just past, I have come to the conclusion that the 1980s was a triumphant decade.

It was a decade that began with the election of Ronald Reagan and ended with a Soviet offer of aid to tranquilize Rumania after the execution of its Communist tyrant. Enough to make us all Whiggish in our reading of history—the eternal optimists. Yes, yes, of course, whenever there is good news, there is the need to remind ourselves that the human predicaments will always be with us. Couéism, so popular in the 1920s ("Every day, in every way, we are getting better and better"), leads to lying down to sleep when the Hitlers of this world, big and small, mobilize their strength. Let the historians hand down final judgments. I, for one, shall forever think of this as Mr. Reagan's decade. No era associated with a single successful leader—not Pericles', not Metternich's, not Victoria's—is fairly evaluated by dredging up surviving delinquencies, deeds left undone. The 1980s are most certainly the decade in which Communism ceased to be a creed, surviving only as a threat. And Ronald Reagan had more to do with this than any other statesman in the world.

Reagan is not Solzhenitsyn. It was Solzhenitsyn who emerged as the Homer of anti-Communism. After the publication of *Gulag*, the European intellectual class could no longer—believe. But *Gulag* notwithstanding, what was beginning to happen, thirty-five years after the end of the Second World War, was sheer accommodationism. We must not doubt the disposition of even civilized people simply to adjust to ugly realities. The Democratic Party leadership dropped its determination to oppose not merely the expansion of the Communist world, but its very being. With the death of Senator Scoop Jackson, steel went out of a great political party. And when the country turned to a new president, and only a few months into his term he pronounced the Soviet Union an "evil empire," the Western diplomatic firmament shook with indignation. How, just how, could a superpower under the leadership of someone who spoke such conclusive words handle the diplomatic challenge of co-existence with that empire? Two years before he left office, the year after the Communists had celebrated the twenty-fifth anniversary of the Berlin Wall, Ronald Reagan was in Berlin, and his words were, "Mr. Gorbachev, tear down this wall!" And then he made that speech in which he especially infuriated the Kremlin by insisting that its system had a rendezvous not with the classless society that was the vision of Marx and Lenin, but with the ash heap of history.

As he spoke, reality was creeping in on Eastern Europe. Before the decade was out we were choking over the wonderful paradoxes, of which the possibility of Soviet troops helping Rumania get rid of a Communist government was perhaps the most spectacular, though my own favorite is Radio Martí, an invention of Ronald Reagan bitterly opposed by American appeasers, broadcasting to Cuba digests of *Moscow News*, which had been banned by Fidel Castro as being too bourgeois.

The great heroes of the decade—Walesa, Solzhenitsyn, Sakharov—have earned their place in freedom's House of Lords; but the political leader was Ronald Reagan, who was trained as a movie actor. Only in America, one is tempted to say; except that Lech Walesa was trained as an electrician.

The Reagan years accustomed us to a mood about life and about government. There were always the interruptions, the potholes of life. But Ronald Reagan had strategic vision. He told us that most of our civic problems were problems brought on or exacerbated by government, not problems that could be solved by government. That of course is enduringly true. Only government can cause inflation, preserve monopoly, and punish enterprise. On the other hand it is only a government leader who can put a stamp on the national mood. One refers not to the period of Shakespeare, but to the period of Elizabeth. Reagan's period was brief, but he did indeed put his stamp on it. He did this in part because he was scornful of the claims of omnipotent government, in part because he felt, and expressed, the buoyancy of the American Republic.

# APPENDIX: SELECTED COLUMNS (AND ONE SPEECH) REFERRED TO IN THE TEXT

## Recall Reagan?

*July 11, 1968*

The movement to recall Governor Ronald Reagan is of little dramatic interest, since it is unlikely that there will be a second act and all but inconceivable that there will be a third act. In order to put recall on the ballot, it is necessary to accumulate 780,414 signatures (i.e., 12 percent of the last vote) on a petition that asks for recall. Anywhere from 30 to 45 percent of such signatures tend to be invalid. So that in order to bring the petition drive to a successful conclusion, well over a million signatures will need to be collected before the end of this month.

The chairman of the recall movement claims to have in hand 650,000 signatures, and it is, to say the least, unlikely that he will double that number in the next three weeks. But let us assume that he does, that there will in fact be a second act. On to the third. What happens then?

There is a lot of false information going the rounds about what Article 23 of the California constitution says. "If [the] current recall campaign gains the needed signatures of 780,000 registered voters by the end of July, the state constitution requires Reagan to step down until a special election can be held," writes the *Berkeley*

*Gazette* (June 22). ". . . If a petition is validated, Governor Reagan will have to turn his job over to Lieutenant Governor Robert Finch for a long as three months—until a special election."

Now that happens to be stuff and nonsense. If the petition is validated, Reagan continues as governor. The only duty that devolves upon the lieutenant governor is cranking up the necessary mechanisms of a special election. As the timetable works out, that election would coincide with the general election of next November. And what then would happen? Why presumably Governor Reagan would win just as he won before. It would take a more idiotic population than California's to turn someone out of office for trying to do what the voters by an emphatic majority showed that they wanted him to do as recently as two years ago. End of story?

Not quite. It is time to ask, Who are the people behind the recall movement, and what shall we think of them? The chairman, Edwin Koupal, is an unemployed car salesman, and you would think that Reagan had signed a state law to the effect that no one could buy a car from Edwin Koupal. Let him pass. The principal organizational support comes from a bunch of labor unions, notably the International Association of Machinists. Let that pass—compulsory labor unions are hardly expected to be practiced in the processes of democratic government.

But then it becomes more interesting. The movement is getting moral encouragement from the intellectual community. A Nobel Prize winner is prominently identified with it. Former Governor Pat Brown has himself signed the petition. The exalted Jesse Unruh is less and "less inclined to oppose a recall." In other words, men who are supposed to know better, indeed men who are professionally engaged in the business of governing, are panting after their own version of Impeach Earl Warren. Exactly the same people who enter the sloughs of despond and wonder about the survival of the human species when anyone mentions the John Birch Society are behaving exactly as that society did in regard to Earl Warren. Last year there was a movement to recall Senator Frank

Church of Idaho. The wailing wall went instantly into action—and quite correctly—pointing out that democracy ought not to work this way. Where is the wailing wall now? Out to lunch.

The California constitution declares that the petition to recall a public official must cite the reason for the recall, but that the reason given is not reviewable. This means, in practical effect, that Governor Reagan could be forced into a special election if 780,414 Californians decided that he was growing bald. The reasons given by the car salesman are not very different: "Ronald Reagan is not competent in matters of government and public affairs" is the first reason given, and the last one, "Ronald Reagan is attempting to further his personal ambitions at the expense of the people in the State of California." As well argue that no one should be permitted to sell cars at the expense of people who buy cars.

The whole idea is to embarrass Reagan. One would think that the liberal community would renounce the backers of this petition before they thoroughly embarrass it.

## Reagan and Nixon
*December 18, 1971*

*Newsweek* carries in the current issue a strangely malevolent story at the expense of Ronald Reagan, Governor of California, the thrust of which is that Reagan is a failure as governor, and that for that reason he has, more or less, thrown himself on the mercies of Richard Nixon.

The writer goes through the usual ritual. Reagan's popularity in the polls is down. That is about as meaningful as the fading of the leaves in the fall, and the ripening buds of spring. A politician's popularity almost always goes down in mid-term, particularly during a second term in office. And in California, where everything is done on an exaggerated scale, from Disneyland to welfare, there is a noisome political situation, a Democratically controlled legislature dominated by an ambitious Speaker of the Assembly who let the legislature go before appropriating the money necessary to balance the state budget. Reagan recalled the legislature, and a tax bill went through. Then, *Newsweek* charges, there is the tarnished image of Governor Reagan, who promised that if he was elected, all the birdies would go tweet tweet tweet. It is true that state costs have risen under Governor Reagan, though only by a small percentage of the rise of the cost of government under his East Coast counterpart, Mayor John V. Lindsay, who promised a $300-million reduction in the cost of government, and proceeded instead to double it.

But Reagan has concentrated, increasingly, on what is benignly called the welfare mess, and has succeeded in making real progress. There are, under his reforms, 140,000 fewer persons in California receiving welfare than last March, notwithstanding that he has had to wrestle with Washington-directed bureaucrats who are fighting for the right of everyone conceivable to live at other people's expense.

The disparagement of Ronald Reagan is, of course, an ideological imperative for those who are dismayed by his questioning of the precepts of contemporary liberalism. But the case against Reagan proves altogether illusory when compared to his actual situation in the contemporary political scene.

"What really irritates Reagan," *Newsweek* reports, "is the recurring rumor that President Nixon no longer really trusts him. His staff is quick to guarantee that Mr. Nixon has no better friend than the governor—which probably provides a clue to Reagan's plans for the future. There are hints that he might seek a Cabinet post or ambassadorship or perhaps oppose Senator Alan Cranston in 1974, though he insists that he is not interested in the Vice Presidency."

The ignorance of the entire paragraph is suggested by the final phrase. If Ronald Reagan were interested in the vice presidency, he would have to be interested in the repeal of the United States Constitution, which specifies that the electoral vote of any given state cannot go to a ticket whose presidential and vice-presidential candidates both come from that state.

"The fact is," says *Newsweek*, "that, unlike in 1968, Reagan now needs Mr. Nixon more than Mr. Nixon needs him." The fact is that that is exactly reversed. Reagan is not running for political office in 1972. Nixon is. And Nixon cannot win the state of California without the enthusiastic endorsement of Ronald Reagan, who, however his constituency is reduced by the vicissitudes of California politics, dominates voters without whom Mr. Nixon is bereft of California.

Or to put it another way, imagine a situation in which Reagan treated Nixon the way Rockefeller treated Goldwater in 1964.

Reagan needs Nixon in a subtle way, unperceived by the opaque treatment of him in *Newsweek*. He needs the federal government to give him a chance to effect reforms in California, free of heavy interference by federal agencies, particularly the Department of Health, Education, and Welfare. The personal insinuations—that Reagan needs Nixon because he wants to be a Cabinet member or an ambassador or a Swiss Guard—are unreal.

If Reagan wants to be a senator, he'll fight a primary, and the White House is not going to

damage him. If he wants to be an ambassador, which is unlikely, it is at most a velleity, hardly the kind of thing for which he would be willing to swap his national constituency, which belongs to him in virtue of his steadfast identification with conservative principle.

## Senator Goldwater's Reassurance

*March 9, 1972*

My friend Senator Goldwater has issued what is in effect a letter to American conservatives, in which he counsels them not to be apprehensive about the Peking summit, nor to heed the "terrible distortions" of the Shanghai communiqué made by "newspaper reporters and news commentators." He informed us that not only has he read the communiqué carefully, as he urges conservatives everywhere to do, he has talked personally to President Nixon and to Mr. Kissinger and to Mr. Rogers,[1] and they reassured him,

---

1. Secretary of State William P. Rogers.

or perhaps at this point we would more accurately say they re-reassured him, that everything is just fine, that nothing has been lost, that we should all be enthusiastic about the Peking summit. Concerning all of which, a few comments:

1. It isn't merely conservative commentators, to whom Mr. Goldwater alludes by indirection, who concluded that Mr. Nixon had, in Peking, substantially altered the traditional U.S. position on Taiwan. Consider, for instance, the dispatch by Mr. Joseph Kraft, the distinguished liberal columnist, written from Shanghai and published in the *Washington Post* on February 29. "The big American loss"— yes, l-o-s-s: and Mr. Kraft read the communiqué very carefully; I know: I was his roommate in Shanghai—"of course, came with respect to Taiwan. The final communiqué . . . makes no mention of the security treaty that binds the United States to support Taiwan against a takeover by force. It was the first time Mr. Nixon himself has climbed down in so explicit a fashion."

Another gentleman who carefully read the communiqué, who is a liberal, who was in China, who is an old China hand, was Mr. Stan Karnow, who wrote in the same issue of the *Washington Post*: "The President's major concession to the Communists was a public pledge for the first time by the United States to withdraw all American forces and military installations from Taiwan. . . . Mr. Nixon acknowledged as well that the United States 'does not challenge' Peking's claim that Taiwan is Chinese territory, and that there is only one China. He further reaffirmed that the Taiwan question should be resolved 'by the Chinese themselves,' thereby emphasizing that the United States no longer bears responsibility for the problem. These U.S. positions thus concede to the Chinese government what it has been requesting for years." I remind Senator Goldwater that Messrs. Kraft and Karnow are not hysterical members of the ultra right.

2. Mr. Goldwater's handling of the troop-withdrawal point is utterly mystifying. What he says is that, after all, "the United States is

always anxious to bring back its forces overseas when conditions warrant, and this goes not only for men and installations stationed on Taiwan but for the men and installations located in Indochina, in Korea, in Europe and elsewhere throughout the world."

Quite so. But what would Senator Goldwater have said if President Nixon had issued a communiqué promising to disband the United States army, navy, and air force, "when conditions warrant"? What would Senator Goldwater have said— indeed what will he say—if Mr. Nixon were to come back from Moscow and tell us that we will withdraw our military forces from Western Europe "as tensions diminish"? Mr. Nixon was either just stating the obvious— that when there are no bad people, there is no need for policemen—or he was saying something that is tactically and strategically significant. In the very same communiqué that Mr. Goldwater manages to suggest the critics of Mr. Nixon haven't read, the Chinese government states: "Wherever there is op-pression, there is resistance. Countries want independence, nations want liberation, and the people want revolution—this has become the irresistible trend of history. The Chinese side expresses its firm support to the peoples of Vietnam, Laos, and Cambodia in their efforts for the attainment of these goals." It pledges, in other words, firm support for subversion everywhere of free governments.

3. If Senator Goldwater doesn't believe that we have made a major concession, of hard psychological substance, he is living in his own world. At Yale University on the day Goldwater spoke, China expert Howard Chao stressed the psychological threat to Nationalist China's security: "Communist China [now] believes it can take Formosa without firing a shot." And Professor H. Bradford Westerfield of the Department of Government concluded that "the demise of Chiang's regime . . . has been brought closer."

It is bad enough to lose Taiwan. The prospect of losing Barry Goldwater is terribly, shatteringly sad.

## Upstaging Reagan

*January 24, 1976*

Parts of President Ford's State of the Union address were clearly drafted at once to harmonize with Ronald Reagan's speeches in New Hampshire and, by playing a soft, reassuring cello, to make Reagan's violin sound screechier and screechier by contrast. Yes, Ford is for a reduction in taxes, like Reagan. Yes, he is in favor of increased state and local responsibility. But it would hardly do—would it, mothers and fathers of America?—to attempt anything that would be disruptive, or to mislead anyone into thinking that social programs come free if they aren't paid for by Congress.

It was a deft maneuver, and Ronald Reagan was more or less expecting it, and knows how to cope with it. Here is the problem he faces: Most states receive money from Washington, D.C., which is, of course, money that originated in the states that are now, suddenly, the beneficiaries of that money. In 1971, for instance, only 9 *percent* of the money "redistributed" through Washington ended up in states different from those whence that money came.

True and radical reform would separate the have states from the have-not states, and once every year or two the richer states would deliberate over the extent of the contributions they are willing to make to the poorer states of the union.

But pending reform at that level, it is necessary to cope with the widespread suspicion that unless you have collective taxation, so to speak, you stand to lose your sources of revenue. Residents of Connecticut—to give an example—are under the impression, in some cases correct, that many of the taxes paid by corporations whose headquarters are in New York, but whose operations are in Connecticut, could go exclusively to New York. They have nightmares about the little office in the Empire State Building, staffed with six executives and ten secretaries, supervising the work of six factories spread along the southern littoral of Connecticut from Stamford to New London, producing an annual profit of $30 million, being taxed now, as matters stand, substantially by the federal government. What if the feds laid off? Wouldn't the state of New York step in and come up with a corporation tax that would take into Albany $15 million a year actually generated in Connecticut?

There are long-term and short-term reforms. The long-term reform would eliminate that kind of tax opportunism, even as it is substantially eliminated by state income taxes levied on the basis of where you actually spend most of your time. But in the meantime, the public is suspicious, and Ronald Reagan should realize this and, accordingly, adjust not his principles but his technique, so as to say: Let the federal government continue as the principal tax collector. But let the federal government reduce its role to that exactly. Let it, having collected the taxes, remit them immediately to the states on a per capita basis, allowing the states to decide the social uses to which these taxes will be put.

This way local government is reinvigorated, cross-state hanky-panky eliminated, and economic sobriety encouraged as the individual congressmen and senators who vote the taxes realize that they are voting for money that was their constituents' to begin with. And the constituents learn gradually the economic facts of life, most relevantly that there isn't very much to be gained from the round trip to which we now subject the welfare dollar.

What Governor Reagan will do, in turn, to curb the excesses of some of Mr. Ford's partisans one cannot predict at this moment. But it will not be a mystery for very long.

## Remarks at the Swearing-In of Evan G. Galbraith
### *November 13, 1981*

Secretary Clark, Jim,[2] Ambassador Galbraith, ladies and gentlemen:

It is characteristic of the personal courage of Ambassador Galbraith that he should have

---

2. Deputy Secretary of State William P. Clark; Under Secretary of State for Security Assistance James L. Buckley.

deputized me to speak on this solemn occasion. Courage, because I have known him for many years, and very well.

But then I have been told that the ceremony here today, to the extent that I figure in it, is *intended* to be highly personal. This was said to me by no fewer than three State Department officials, from which I deduce that there was some active concern in these parts that I might take the occasion to recite my Weltanschauung. To do so would be in the tradition of those journalists who do not report events without giving historical background. We recall that the lead sentence in the London *Times* announcing the declaration of war against the Kaiser began: "Back in 1870 . . ."

Well, if it is to be personal history, so be it.

Back in 1948, it happened that I won the only election I ever won. I remember having called my brother Jim, at the time a student at the Yale Law School, while I was a sophomore in the undergraduate school. I had expected that the voting for the chairmanship of the Yale *Daily News*, which

election was traditionally carried out one year before assumption of office, would be close. Since Jim had been an officer of the newspaper, I asked him whether it would be ethical for me to vote—on the unsigned ballot we each would insert into the basket—for myself. Jim, then as now, believed in deliberation; but he told me that, yes, he thought this could be done discreetly, and in good conscience. And so the following day I folded the piece of paper with my own name written on it and dropped it in with the other twenty or thirty. A few minutes later the incumbent chairman emerged, and announced that I had been elected the chairman of the Yale *Daily News* for 1949–50. He paused dramatically and smiled, adding, "I am pleased to report that Bill was elected unanimously."

We moved, a few of us, from that chamber to the nearest watering hole, which was Deke fraternity house, and there a blond, heavyset fellow sophomore accosted me to ask, with what I came to know as characteristic curiosity and ebullience, just what was the hilarity all about. It is something of a poetical miracle that, thirty-three years later, I should be involved in a situation that calls for at least as much hilarity. The similarities are almost perfect. It is rumored that Van voted for himself. And the president has told me that the vote for Van was unanimous.

I have not confided to the president, or to Secretary Clark, or to anybody, I guess, my special knowledge of the general and orderly deliberation given by Van Galbraith to the hypothetical possibility of joining the government.

It happens that in June a year and a half ago, when the president was still only a candidate for the Republican nomination, Van and I were together, as I am happy to say we have often been, on a sailboat. I have in mind a conversation we had about two hundred miles south of Bermuda, heading first for that island, then on to the Azores, then to Spain. There were six of us doing the sailing and the navigating. The day was blue, the wind brisk; we were an entire happy day removed from a sloppy and emetic little storm that had dogged us for forty-eight hours. As we were eating lunch, one of our company, Dick Clurman—former head of correspondents for Time-Life, and former commissioner of parks and cultural affairs in New York City—was arguing the nobility and inspiration of public service. As I remember, I was somewhat skeptical, adhering to a rather dogmatic position that there was a deep and instinctive antagonism between service in the private and in the public sectors. Van, if I remember, joined in expressing skepticism of a sort, reminiscing briefly about his single experience in public service, as aide to a secretary of commerce in the Eisenhower administration. If memory serves, the conversation was not extended, lasting only for three or four minutes, but the banter did indicate something of the mood of the freshly installed ambassador to France, back in the long ago, when there was another president in the White House, and when the only immediate problem Van Galbraith faced was whether the navigator would succeed in guiding the boat to Bermuda. . . .

[At this point WFB gestured to a confederate, and a television screen was unveiled in a corner of the room. A videotape from the documentary that had been made of that Atlantic crossing came on the screen. As WFB wrote in *Overdrive*, "It showed the ketch in full sail, Clurman and Galbraith heatedly arguing in the cockpit, Galbraith insisting that working for the government was generally pointless. He recalled his own experience as a legal aide to the secretary of commerce. The last words the audience heard him utter were: 'Don't you understand, Dick, most of the people in Washington are *assholes*.' The crowd roared, the screen went blank."]

For the first years of their marriage, Van and Bootsie lived in Paris. They came back, briefly, to America for a year in New York, after which they were gone again, this time to London, where for a number of years he pursued his professional career [as a banker-lawyer], traveling frequently to New York and spending his vacation periods for the most part in Switzerland, where on his first visit I took him skiing for the first time,

forgetting in my informal instructions to tell him how a skier goes about arresting his forward motion, resulting in brief companionship at the top of the mountain, followed by a descent which might have been the closing scene of a Marx Brothers movie called *An Afternoon on the Mountain*. As I think back on it, if I were to add the distances we have sailed together to the distances we have skied together, it is probably safe to say that we have, by wind and gravity, circled the globe.

It was at law school at Harvard that Van first interested himself in the politics that make the world go round, so very eccentrically. Soon he became conversant with the principal engines of political behavior, and with those forces that have pockmarked this century. I remember once, in 1957, when we found ourselves in Baltimore to serve as ushers at the wedding of a friend, and in the morning I thought impulsively to visit Whittaker Chambers in Westminster, one hour away. One would not take just anyone to that reclusive eyrie in western Maryland, but I took Van there with full confidence, and we stayed two hours. A few days later I had a letter from Chambers. He began it, "I liked Galbraith at sight. This happens so seldom with me that I wondered why it happened. As I listened to him laugh, watched him study the titles of my books, watched his mind fasten on one or two points of no great importance in themselves, but somewhat as an ant, at touch, clamps on the rib of a leaf that may be littering its path, I liked him better. I decided that what I liked was a kind of energy, what kind scarcely mattered. One of our generals was once being ho-ho-hearty with the ranks, as I understand generals are sometimes, especially if newsmen are present. He asked a paratrooper, 'Why do you like to do an insane thing like jumping out of airplanes?' The paratrooper answered: 'I don't like to, sir, I just like to be around the kind of people who like to jump out of airplanes.' I felt something like the paratrooper about Galbraith. . . ."

His friends, for whom I speak, would agree that his qualities are special. Everyone who has known him is more cheerful for the experience of having known him. The French will find him, in his official capacity, in no sense different from how they found him in private life fifteen years ago. He is hospitable to every kind of ambiguity, charitable in his constructions of human behavior, but entirely convinced that the Lord has provided man with a fundamental apparatus by which we distinguish between what is right and what isn't; and convinced that the challenge to right thought and right conduct was never in history more menacingly posed. I can imagine no presence in Paris more distinctively American than Van's, because jaded and worldly men will see in him the storybook American, the man of spontaneity and steadfastness, of innocence and wit, of flexibility and purpose. It may seem somehow wrong, in these circumstances, to congratulate the French people, but exactly that far I am prepared to go, confident as all of us who have known him over the years are, as also those of you in government who have known him over the years or have come recently to know him— Al Haig, Bill Clark, Bill Draper, Tom Clausen, Tom Enders, Jim

Buckley, Jack Maresca, my son Christopher—that his presence as his country's ambassador will inform and refresh, yet another installment in the apparently endless repayment of the debt we incurred when, as a young and struggling republic, we welcomed the arrival of Lafayette. I join you all in wishing him and Bootsie a great and fruitful adventure, in the service of our beloved country.

## Understanding Reagan
*April 24, 1986*

When Henry Kissinger went down to Washington last week to address a meeting of academics at what he thought was a closed meeting, he spoke of Ronald Reagan and his administration in terms he would not have used addressing a Republican rally. But if you listened carefully to everything Kissinger said, and weighed it comprehensively, you would find it much more shocking to academics than to Reagan loyalists.

Of Ronald Reagan, Kissinger said that, just to clear the air, he was

in no way "indebted" to Reagan—in the sense, let us say, that Henry Kissinger would be bound to acknowledge being indebted to Richard Nixon. He went on: Moreover, if you meet Reagan and talk with him briefly, you wonder how he managed to be elected governor of California, let alone president of the United States.

One can hear the academic audience purring at this point; but it did not anticipate what was to come. Kissinger went on to say that in fact Reagan had dominated the politics of California for eight years, had dominated the political life of the United States for six years, and not inconceivably could go down as one of the most significant presidents of the century.

How can this be?

Because, Kissinger explained, the apparent limitations of Reagan totally disguise an intuitive grasp he has not only for priorities, but also for technique. Here, Kissinger later explained, is a man who managed to change his entire staff without a ripple of change in policy, so clearly did he himself dominate policy. And here is a president who outwitted the Soviet Union through 1983 and 1984 on the matter of deploying theater nuclear weapons in Europe. When Gorbachev arrived in Geneva it was widely conjectured that he would eat Reagan alive. But Reagan's intuitive wit, his sense of what to get into, what not to get into—what academics might call his reticulative sense of order—ended him up dominating the summit. And just as Gorbachev now believes that by threatening a summit cancellation because of Libya he will embarrass Reagan, quite the contrary is likely: Gorbachev will lose, and Reagan gain.

Now what got reported from all the above over ABC was mostly the business about how Kissinger wondered that Reagan ever got elected governor of California, let alone president of the United States. Nothing was said about the subtleties of Mr. Kissinger's extemporized remarks, let alone his statement to the academics that they tend to suffer as a class because academics tend nowadays to be either job-seekers or revolutionaries. They are, accordingly, not at-

tempting to carry the load, to help public figures to conceptualize problems with clarity. As an example, take Nicaragua. Mr. Reagan is here genuinely handicapped by his rendering of the problem. Either the problem is grave enough to bring about U.S. action, or it is not. If it is, $100 million is a meaningless antitoxin; if it is not, then we have no business helping the Contras at all. The academic class tends to ignore refinements in stating the question.

One notes from Ronald Reagan Jr.'s amusing and deft piece in *Playboy* magazine that alongside the son-reporter, hiding outside the summit room in Geneva, was presidential historian Edmund Morris, with the same numinous notepad on which he has written the first part of the best biography ever done on Theodore Roosevelt. It is Kissinger's implicit point that Reagan deserves a biographer of the subtlety of Morris. But between now and the consolidation of Reagan's reputation in America's history, commentators need to be cautious. Last year, Jack Kemp's press aide, John Buckley (a nephew of mine), bunted a question about Kemp (Wasn't he too stupid to be president?) by citing Reagan (They said Reagan was too stupid to be president). What emerged in many news stories was merely: Kemp Aide Says Reagan Too Stupid to Be President.

Ronald Reagan is a very unusual man, with unusual habits of mind and manner. Four months ago, a retiring and shy editor was asked by a friend whether she had been apprehensive at the prospect of sitting for two and one-half hours next to the president of the United States at the formal dinner. "Well," she said, "as a matter of fact I was. But as soon as he sat down, he turned to me and said, 'Priscilla, do you want to hear what I said to Gorbachev?'"

You wonder how such a man as that can get elected governor of California. But then you think about it for a while, and you find yourself wondering how come, the last time the voters were consulted, that man won only 49 states.

## The Effort to Intimidate Reagan
*June 30, 1987*

If the ideological opportunists get away with this one, we may as well abandon hope—democracy, in the language of the flower children, sucks.

They bring in Professor Laurence Tribe all the way from Frankfurt, West Germany, to tell us why President Reagan should not nominate to the Supreme Court a judicial scholar whose views of the responsibilities of the court are similar to those of Ronald Reagan. And here is what Professor Tribe comes up with: Waal, he says, it's this way. Up until now, the court has been balanced between conservatives and liberals. When last summer Mr. Reagan named Antonin Scalia to the seat of William Rehnquist (who was nominated to fill the seat of chief justice, vacated by Warren Burger), that was okay, because Reagan was sending in a true-blue conservative to replace a true-blue conservative.

But what is now happening is that a moderate is quitting the bench—Mr. Justice Lewis Powell. It is clearly the responsibility of the president to name a moderate to fill that vacancy.

Question: But how is that so, Professor, since the president is supposed to name people he thinks would do the best job in interpreting the Constitution?

Aha! Professor Tribe is very glad you asked that question. Clearly you have forgotten that the Constitution gives the president the authority to nominate but also gives the Senate the right to advise and consent. And the Senate doesn't want a series of delicate questions that have in recent years been decided in one way by a 5–4 vote, Mr. Powell providing the swing vote, to be undone by a new majority. That would simply be an abdication of the Senate's right to advise and consent.

But—but Mr. Tribe, if there is no questioning the reputability of the candidate chosen by the president, aren't you applying a litmus test in the choice of judicial candidates, which is what the Democratic Party so roundly denounced at its last convention?

Tribe does not much like that question and goes back to his theory that President Reagan must not wrench from the American people hard-won rights.

The sad aspect of all the sophistry being used is that it strengthens the point many Americans have been fretting over with increasing anxiety for more than a generation. It is that the Supreme Court has become the supreme legislative chamber, and that although the Constitution gives only to Congress the right to enact legislation, and only to the people and their legislatures the right to amend the Constitution, the Supreme Court has been busy doing all of these things with abandon since the days of the Warren Court and even before. The intensity of the current fight has to do with whether President Reagan will appoint someone to the court whose vote might reverse one-man majorities on such questions as abortion, school prayer, affirmative action, and the rights of defendants.

Ronald Reagan was elected president having made his views

plain on everything from the United Nations to weeping willow trees. And his position on the Supreme Court is inherently consistent. Either legislate a change in the nation's legal folkways and mores, or else restore to the court a majority that will refrain from usurping the responsibilities of Congress. To make that determination sound as though Mr. Reagan were engaged in personally overthrowing the views of the founding fathers on inflamed social questions is a forensic sleight of hand qualifying anyone who uses it as Distinguished Mouthpiece of Constitutional Evasion.

It's worth while dwelling on a hypothetical case. Let us suppose that tomorrow the Supreme Court ruled 5–4 that smoking a cigarette was a homicidal act (the court has engaged in reasoning equally venturesome). One of the justices constituting the majority resigns, and the president nominates to replace him someone who, among other things, does not believe that the Fifth Amendment's guarantee against the taking of life except under due process of law requires

the prohibition of tobacco. Is the president who names this candidate to the court engaged in a covert maneuver to re-license tobacco, or is he engaged in appointing to the court a man whose constitutional judgment he has confidence in?

It is not surprising that the liberals in America, having trained the Supreme Court to act as a standing constitutional convention, are frightened to death that they may lose control of their Big Bertha. Mr. Reagan has the best opportunity of his administration to fight for constitutional rectitude.

## A Farewell to the Reagans
*January 17, 1989*
The portrait of Ronald and Nancy Reagan done by Mike Wallace for *60 Minutes* was their envoi to the republic on their leaving the White House. And this is mine to them.

The whole thing seems a cheerful mix of nostalgia and ephemera, but the portrait was genuine and will be studied (or should be) by future biographers.

What will Nancy miss the most about the White House? (Long pause. Furrowed brow. Let me see, now. She looks up, as though she had discovered the key to world peace.) "Well, when you want a plumber, you have a plumber."

And Ron baby. "Is it true that when you get the papers in the morning the first thing you read is the funny pages, then the sports pages, and only then the national and international news?" (Hard, attentive look. He might have been asked whether he would give up SDI in return for a 50 percent reduction in Soviet ICBMs.) "That's true about the funny pages. But not about the sports page. I haven't had the time for that." The burdens of office.

The net effect of it is to stimulate in the reader not contempt for such habits, but a very bad conscience for those of us who are missing out on the funny pages. It's there that the day-to-day character of American thought is most vividly transcribed, the president seems to be telling us, without being didactic about it.

He goes on. "I am a voracious reader. My idea of Hades" (Note: not his idea of "hell." This is the president who once spoke of being up to his "keister.") "is to find myself in a hotel room without a book to read."

"Well, what book are you now reading?"

The audience expects now to hear him say, "Oh, *Being and Nothingness*," or maybe "*The Critique of Pure Reason*." He tells us, "George Burns's book about Gracie." Ronald Reagan would not engage in affectation to storm the gates of heaven.

What about the charge that your administration has been indifferent to the problems of racism? Why, racism, all forms of prejudice were the most despicable of sins where he grew up.

"But many black leaders charge you with it."

The shrewd Ronald Reagan takes this on. "Sometimes I wonder if they really want what they say they want, because some of those leaders are doing very well." Translation: Some black leaders have a vested interest in the stimulation of complaints about racism.

That statement is as true as it is that some people in fact live off the high incidence of cancer. . . .

Well, but who, exactly, are you talking about? Jesse Jackson?

The shrewd RR will go only so far. "I'll let you name them."

What about his reaction to Soviet leader Mikhail Gorbachev? "Well, I'll tell you. My people said if we could leave Reykjavik with one more summit scheduled, that would make Reykjavik a success. So he and I sat down and I said, Let's take a walk, and during that walk I said to him, You know, we don't distrust each other because we have arms, we have arms because we distrust each other. And then I said, You've never been in America, and he said, You've never been in Russia. So I said, Will you come to America for the next summit? And he said, Yes, I agree. And he said, Next year, you come to Moscow? And I said, I agree. When I got back and told my people we had just arranged for two more summits, they couldn't believe it."

Did he think there was a spiritual side to Gorbachev? "Well, he used the word God a lot and I wondered about that, but I checked with my people and they said that it was just a figure of speech, you know, God with a small *g*."

This didn't surprise Nancy. She went on to say that Raisa Gorbachev was a "convinced Marxist." Had there been tension between her and Raisa? Well, "She was as nervous as I was."

What was Nancy's happiest day during the presidency? "The day Ronnie left the hospital." Nancy's hand glides over, and rests now over his. What was the president's happiest time during his political years? Well, the question reminded him of something Clark Gable once said, which is that the happiest sound in the world is that of the footsteps of the one you love approaching the other side of the door. "That's the way I feel about Nancy."

No farewell to the Reagans could more appropriately close than by quoting the final paragraphs of Whittaker Chambers's *Witness*. "One of the tenderest of Greek fables tells how the gods decided to go down to the earth as beggars to try the charity of men. The god Hermes, clad in rags, knocked at many prosperous doors and was driven from each. Toward evening, he came to the meanest door of all, a mere hut, where two old people, Philemon and Baucis, his wife, tended a few vines and milked their goats. Hermes knocked there. Because his need touched them, the old people took him in. They shared their meal with him, and, at night, let him sleep on the floor before their fire, trusting to their poverty and their age to prevent any harm that the beggar might intend.

"In the morning, Hermes asked each of the old people to name his most secret wish, supposing that it would be for longer life, gold, or great flocks. The dearest wish of each turned out to be the same—that both might die, as they had lived, together, that neither might die first, for neither could endure to face what remained of a life that would be unendurable without the other.

"The god, now gleaming through his rags, raised his staff— the caduceus with the twined snakes, interlacing good and evil.

Where Philemon and Baucis had stood, two trees rustled up whose branches met and touched when the wind blew."

## The Democrats Win with a Sweep

*April 9, 1991*

It was a great weekend for the tabs, opening day of the season for (1) baseball and (2) scandal dueling. The Democrats' key players were Senator Ted Kennedy, his son Patrick, and his nephew Willie Smith. Representing the Republicans, there was Nancy Reagan, with Ronald Reagan and others playing bit parts. As a partisan, I regretfully report that the Democrats are way, way ahead, based on opening-day performances.

The Republicans suffer, for one thing, from lack of contemporaneity. What was allegedly done by the Democratic team is extremely current, whereas the Republicans came up with events some of which were between three and eleven years old, most of which were forty years old, making the producer of the Republican show, Kitty Kelley, sound a little like Suetonius, who wrote about the sex lives of the Caesars and who died about 1,900 years ago.

The Democratic team came in with a singular advantage, what the dramatists call the mise-en-scène, the background time and place. It was Good Friday, the most solemn day in the Christian calendar. And it is not disputed that the Democratic star, Senator Kennedy, chose this day to celebrate at the bar. Right on past midnight, until 3 o'clock in the morning. That's the hour when the bar closes, so he and his supporting cast invited a barmaid and another lady to accompany them home for another drink. Another drink at 3 a.m. is a high act of redundancy by most people's standards. On the other hand, it's also something that generates great audience suspense.

Besides, there are those who admire that grim tenacity with which some Democratic players hang in there, right to the very, very end.

And then, of course, there was the "episode." Live theater. Followed by the disappearance, or so it would seem, of the Palm Beach police. This added greatly to the dramatic effect: The three principal players just walked off the scene, unnoticed, unquestioned, not even stopping for the applause of the crowd. That takes some stagecraft. And the principal player, identified by the tragic heroine of the evening as the tortfeasor, wouldn't even talk with the police when they finally materialized. All he would do is volunteer specimens of his hair and a drop or two of his blood.

The audience, coast to coast, was wild with excitement as Act One of the Kennedy saga closed, and the anticipation for Act Two is enormous.

Meanwhile, producer Kitty Kelley did her very best with Nancy Reagan as her star. She began by saying that forty years ago Nancy Reagan advanced her date of birth by two years. This was not a very successful line, and the yawns in the house set Ms. Kelley's teeth on edge. So she said that Mrs. Reagan had been pregnant when she married her husband. But that was not a very big theatrical deal, it turned out, because the fact had been revealed in Mrs. Reagan's own autobiography over a year ago. The audience wanted much more.

So Ms. Kelley said that both the Reagans were, as they would put it in Hollywood, "socially active" before their marriage. With that news, Ms. Kelley was almost blown off the stage. Socially active before they were married! Had Ms. Kelley never read the Kinsey Report, which was published about the time the Reagans were being socially active? The crowd became very nearly mutinous, but Ms. Kelley went doggedly on.

She shot her Big Bertha: Frank Sinatra. His name brought silence to the house. It is a very big name for Ms. Kelley, because she wrote an entire book about him, portraying him as having engaged in activities that, well, activities that . . . well, bring up the subject with your doctor, if you see what I mean.

But now she tried to convince the audience that when the president of the United States was out of town, Nancy would invite Frank Sinatra to the White House,

close all the doors, block all the telephone lines, instruct the operators not even to put the president through to her when he called, and there, between 12:30 and 3:30, she would have at it with Frank Sinatra.

The audience began to smile. A little bit of that same smile you spotted a couple of years ago when Bob Woodward wrote his book about Bill Casey and said that Casey had called him into the hospital room a few minutes or hours or a day or two before Casey died, and there confessed to Woodward everything he had done wrong, everything President Reagan had done wrong, everything the CIA had done wrong, plus he once forgot his morning prayers and missed Mass on a holy day of obligation.

A look of skepticism overtook the audience, and Ms. Kelley was heard to say to a close collaborator, who insists on anonymity, that next time she is going to play on the Democratic team, who are much, much better at this kind of thing.

# INDEX

ABC, 46n2, 138n2, 194, 257
ABM treaty. *See* Anti-Ballistic Missile
(ABM) treaty
ACU. *See* American Conservative
Union
ADA. *See* Americans for Democratic
Action
Afghanistan
"ambassadorship" to, 139, 145,
157, 158, 161, 162, 166, 170,
174, 195, 198, 203, 213–214,
231, 236
potential confrontation over, 118
war in, 180
Agnew, Spiro, 61, 69, 73, 165
resignation of, 60–61n7
AIDS sufferers, identifying marks on,
196
*Airborne* (Buckley), 86n4
Airline safety, 83
Air-traffic controllers, dealing with, 124
Allen, Gracie, 261
American Book Award, 208
American Conservative Union (ACU),
85, 85n2
*American Life, An* (Reagan), 217, 219

Americans for Democratic Action
(ADA), 75, 85n2, 192, 193
Anderson, John, 148
Anderson, Martin, 231
Annenberg, Leonore, 158
*Answered Prayers* (Capote), 31
Anti-Ballistic Missile (ABM) treaty,
197, 197n5, 198, 199
Anti-Communism, 58, 75, 197, 240
Anti-Semitism, 173, 232
Aquinas, St. Thomas, 183
*Arabia, the Gulf, and the West* (Kelly),
139n5
Arizona state penitentiary, Capote at,
31
Ashbrook, John, 55n1
Astaire, Fred, 89, 174
Astor, Brooke, 141
*Atlantic, The:* Stockman and, 148, 149
*Atlantic High* (Buckley), 142n8

Bach, Johann Sebastian, 191, 234
Baker, Howard, 164, 164n3
Balanced budgets, 123, 147, 155
Social Security and, 150
Barry, David, 232

Stein, Jules, 58
Stewart, Potter, 145
Stockman, David
  budget and, 147–150
  economic scene and, 148
  problems with, 148–149,
    157–158, 164
  Reaganomics and, 149–150
Strategic Defense Initiative (SDI), 190,
  197, 197n5, 201, 221, 261
  debate over, 205–206
Strikes, dealing with, 124
Suetonius, 264
Sumner, Gordon, Jr., 114

Taft, Robert, 75
Taiwan (Formosa), 109, 167, 168,
  248–249
Taxes, 154, 162
  capital-gains, 119, 120
  cutting, 121, 122, 123, 148,
    157–158, 160–161, 162
  estate, 68
  federal government and, 21, 22,
    250–251
  income, 23, 26, 68, 120, 121,
    122
  on interest/savings, 119, 122
Taylor, Kathleen "Babe" (WFB's
  mother-in-law), 60
Tenth Amendment, 123
Thanksgiving, 77–80, 229
Thatcher, Margaret, 138, 138n4,
  195n4, 232, 237
Thatcher Institute, 232
Thirty Years' War, 78
Thomas, Clarence, 232
Thurber, James, 107
Thurmond, Strom, 41–42, 74
Time Inc., 36
*Time* magazine, 237
*Times* (London), 217, 252
Timothy Dwight college (Yale), 222
Tito, Josip Broz, 117

*Today Show*, 171
Torrijos, Omar, 86n3, 87, 97, 97n2,
  103, 104, 208n15
*Treasure Island* (Stevenson), 19
Tribe, Laurence, 258–260
Truman, Harry, 75
Tureck, Rosalyn, 191, 194
Twain, Mark, 25, 26
22nd Amendment, 205, 208, 214, 215

Unemployment, 25, 120, 147, 233
  inflation and, 148
Unicameral legislature, Reagan and,
  64–65
Unions, dealing with, 75, 124
United States Advisory Commission on
  Information, 48
U.S. Air Arena, 235
U.S. Constitution, 175, 179, 220, 246,
  259
  federal government and, 123
U.S. Department of Commerce, 120
U.S. Department of Defense, 70
U.S. Department of Education, 123
U.S. Department of Health, Education,
  and Welfare, 247
U.S. Justice Department, 208n15
U.S. Marines, 200
United States Post Office, 174
U.S. State Department, speech at, 158,
  251–256
United States Steel Company, 121
U.S. Supreme Court, 25, 220, 260
  selections for, 127, 144–145, 203,
  258–259
University of Southern California,
  award from, 47
Unruh, Jesse, 18–19, 244, 245
*Up from Liberalism* (Buckley), 4, 204

Vanderbilt University, lecture at,
  185–186
*Vanity Fair*, 174
Vaughn, Robert, 33n1

**William F. Buckley Jr.** (1925–2008) was an intellectual leader of the Right for more than fifty years. The founder and editor-in-chief of *National Review* and founder and host of *Firing Line*, he was also the author of more than fifty books of fiction and nonfiction. His syndicated column, "On the Right," was begun in 1962 and appeared in newspapers around the country for forty-six years. He served (briefly) as a CIA agent in the early 1950s, helped found Young Americans for Freedom in 1960, and was awarded the Presidential Medal of Freedom by George H. W. Bush in 1991. He died in February 2008.